MW00720079

VANISHED
The Michael Dunahee Story

by VALERIE GREEN

hancock
house

ISBN 978-0-88839-725-6

Library and Archives Canada Cataloguing in Publication

Green, Valerie
    Vanished : the Michael Dunahee story / by Valerie Green.

    Includes bibliographical references and index.
    Issued also in electronic format.
    ISBN 978-0-88839-725-6

    1. Dunahee, Michael, 1986– —Kidnapping, 1991. 2. Dunahee, Michael, 1986–
—Family. 3. Missing children—Family relationships—British Columbia—Victoria.
4. Kidnapping victims—Psychology. 5. Kidnapping victims—British Columbia—Victoria.
6. Kidnapping—British Columbia—Victoria. 7. Missing persons—Registers. I. Title.

HV6762.C3G74 2012   364.15'4092   C2012-906437-8

Editor: Theresa Laviolette
Production: Ingrid Luters
Cover Design: Ingrid Luters

*We acknowledge the financial support of the Government of Canada through the
Canada Book Fund for our publishing activities.*

Printed in Canada—KROMAR

Published simultaneously in Canada and the United States by
HANCOCK HOUSE PUBLISHERS LTD.
19313 Zero Avenue, Surrey, BC Canada V3S 9R9
1431 Harrison Avenue, Blaine, WA, USA 98230-5005
(604) 538-1114 Fax (604) 538-2262

www.hancockhouse.com | sales@hancockhouse.com

For Michael

and for missing children everywhere

The missing children awareness ribbon is green—the colour of hope. It symbolizes light in the darkness and is an expression of our thoughts for missing children, their families and friends.

—From the website of Child Find BC,
commemorating National Missing Children's Day,
May 25th each year

GREEN RIBBON DAY

In 1986, the Solicitor General of Canada declared May 25th to be National Missing Children's Day in Canada. The Green Ribbon of Hope is recognized as a symbol to help remember missing children and to seek their safe return. It is also used as an expression of our thoughts for missing children, their families and friends. Activities carried out during the month include fingerprinting clinics and various community fundraisers.

The concept of the Green Ribbon of Hope was originated by the students and faculty of Holy Cross Secondary School in St. Catherine's, Ontario, following the abduction and subsequent murder of fifteen-year-old Kristen French. Her classmates came to Child Find to ask us to develop a legacy for Kristen and all missing children in Canada.

Each May, Child Find hosts the Green Ribbon of Hope campaign. During the month of May, community members are asked to show their support and concern for the issue of missing children by prominently wearing a green ribbon. Proceeds generated by the campaign enable Child Find BC to continue its mandate of assisting in the search process for missing children and the education of children and adults about child safety.

Contents

Foreword 7

Author's First Word 9

Introduction: A Portrait of Victoria 11

Chapter 1:   Sunday, March 24, 1991 15

Chapter 2:   The First Two Months 20

Chapter 3:   The Initial Leads 30

Chapter 4:   Keeping the Hope Alive 38

Chapter 5:   Child Find 51

Chapter 6:   The Media Challenge 55

Chapter 7:   No Reprieve 81

Chapter 8:   The Twentieth Anniversary Year 89

Chapter 9:   Sister in the Shadow 95

Chapter 10: Life Since 1991 101

Chapter 11: Never Stop Believing 112

Chapter 12: A Letter to Michael 121

Conclusion 124

Author's Last Word 128

Appendices

I. AMBER Alert System and GPS 131

II. Safety Tips from Child Find. 135

III. National Child Exploitation Co-ordination Centre 143

IV. Missing Children's Day in the United States 147

V. Children's Bill of Rights 150

VI. Child Find Offices 151

Bibliography 153

Sources 154

Index 156

Acknowledgements 158

About the Author 160

Foreword

It has now been over twenty-one years since the community of Victoria, British Columbia was shaken to its foundation with the news that a four-year-old boy was missing. He was just an ordinary little boy from an ordinary working class family in a time when parents rarely had to worry about the abduction of their children. All of this changed on March 24, 1991. This was a moment in time when a community changed forever; when a family faced every parent's worst nightmare.

Growing up in Victoria or in countless other communities across Canada and around the world, we can recall our childhoods as a time of exploration, adventure and play in neighborhoods where there was a feeling that we all looked out for one another and that we were safe. Since 1991 our societal values and norms have changed; many parents no longer feel that same safety of community that was once a given. We now need to educate our children on safety, abuse, bullying and exploitation. Childhood in many respects will never be the same as it once was.

What has happened to the Dunahee family since 1991 is the most remarkable thing of all. Despite the grief and horror of their son Michael's disappearance, and then on through their years of searching, activism, involvement and support for other families with missing children, to becoming a family that is constantly in the public eye provincially, nationally and internationally, the Dunahees have somehow managed to remain intact. In fact, they have survived and grown.

This story is about tragedy, strength and resolve in the face of unimaginable adversity; and it is also about the fact that today we all share a common vision, that through hope and faith we can build a better future for our children and a place where our kids are safe and communities care. It is a story that definitely needed to be told. Author Valerie Green has undertaken this challenge with sensitivity and respect for all those concerned.

The search for Michael Dunahee continues today and will carry on until we bring Michael home. We simply can't give up because the memory of Michael's disappearance and the hope of finding him are far too important, and that hope is what keeps the Dunahee family and the community strong.

— STEVE ORCHERTON
Executive Director Child Find BC

Author's First Word

The book you are about to read has no ending. The reason for this will soon become apparent.

Unfortunately, there can be no ending to this tragic story until the person involved in the disappearance of Michael Dunahee on March 24, 1991 comes forward and confesses. There might be others who saw something that day and still have a long-hidden memory that could be the missing link or the one necessary lead enabling the police investigation to be solved, thereby bringing closure to this case—and, thus, an ending to this book. There might also be someone out there who knows who took Michael and, for reasons unknown, has refused to disclose the truth.

Whatever transpired on that day, there will never of course be complete closure for the Dunahee family who lost a child, a brother, a grandchild, a nephew and a little friend. They have been deprived of seeing Michael grow from a sweet child into a young man. Even if he were to return to them today, they can never recapture those lost years and all that they have missed in between.

This book tells the story of Michael's family and how losing their son in March 1991 has changed their lives. And, it is the story of how they have managed to survive for over two decades living on hope that has never diminished. Some may say that after so many years have passed it is false hope. Others disagree and feel only admiration for the strength and dedication the Dunahees have shown throughout the years, and how they have turned their own personal tragedy into a public triumph.

With the family's permission, I have told their complete story, including the good and the bad. No one could have come through that horrendous event without some scars, an event that left a legacy of broken hearts, damaged relationships and paths taken which were not those the family would have wanted. But somehow, against all odds, the Dunahees have carried on and made a new life without a son whose memory is always with them. It is not the life they would have chosen, but it is now the only life they know.

The narrative is also peppered throughout with information about other missing children cases—of which there are many—with comparisons and attempts to give hope and inspiration to all those who are still seeking closure.

This book, however, is mostly Michael's story. It is the tragic tale of a small boy whose true identity was stolen from him.

So, if you read this book and know something—anything—that would give this story an ending, please do not hesitate any longer. Unburden yourself from a secret you have held for well over two decades. Someone, somewhere knows the truth. You might consider disclosing your secret after you read how your action (or lack there-of) on that fateful day has shattered the life of one family and held them captive in a time capsule of despair and unanswered questions for so many years.

The Dunahees, the police, Child Find, the Missing Children's Society and the author of this book, beg you to give the answers needed. It is as simple as making one phone call with the truth to any of the following three numbers or to any of the numbers listed at the end of this book in the Appendices.

Victoria Police Tip-Line: 250-995-7444 or 250-995-7654

Crimestoppers: 1-800-222-8477

Child Find BC: 250-382-7311 or (no charge) 1-888-689-3463

Introduction
A portrait of Victoria, British Columbia

In order to set the scene of Michael's abduction, something should first be known about the area of Greater Victoria.

The capital city of Victoria is located on the southern tip of Vancouver Island just off the west coast of Canada. It is situated approximately 100 kilometers (sixty-two miles) from BC's largest city of Vancouver on the mainland, and is also the same distance away by airplane or ferry from Seattle, Washington, in the United States. A mere forty kilometers (twenty-five miles) separates Victoria from Port Angeles, Washington, by ferry across the Juan de Fuca Strait. In 1991, with a population of just under 70,000 and a crime rate that was relatively low when compared to other major cities across North America, there was nothing particularly remarkable about the city. Victoria was then, and still is, known mostly for its beauty and its friendliness. Described as "a little bit of olde England" or "the City of Gardens," it is a place that enjoys an easy-going lifestyle.

But what happened in March of 1991 year shook Victoria to the core and altered the complacency of its residents forever. It also spotlighted the city across Canada, North America and around the world for all the wrong reasons.

That tragic incident might well have happened in any city in Canada or North America. Similar incidents of missing and abducted children have indeed occurred in other places; but the one in Victoria was soon to become one of Canada's largest-ever missing persons' investigations—and consequently one of the most frustrating for investigators. At the centre of that tragedy was the Dunahee family whose four-year-old son, Michael, was stolen from them in a split second just metres away from where they stood. The chances of such a kidnapping happening are one in 100,000. Over twenty years later, Michael's whereabouts are still unknown.

Named for Queen Victoria of the United Kingdom, Victoria is one of the oldest cities in the Pacific Northwest, with British settlement starting in 1841. That was the year when James Douglas of the Hudson's Bay Company founded Fort Victoria, describing the area as "a perfect Eden." Coast Salish First Nations people had established communities in that area several thousand years earlier, long before non-native settlement.

Victoria became the central port and main outfitting centre for miners en route to the Fraser Canyon gold fields when gold was first discovered on the BC mainland in 1858. This caused the city's population to rise from little more than 500 to well over 5,000 within a few days. In 1862, the city was incorporated and in 1865 Esquimalt became the North Pacific home of the Royal Navy, remaining Canada's west coast naval base to this day.

In 1866, Victoria was designated as the capital of the newly united colony, instead of New Westminster; this was not a popular decision with those living on the mainland. When British Columbia joined the Canadian Confederation in 1871, Victoria officially became the provincial capital.

By the latter half of the nineteenth century, the Port of Victoria had become one of North America's largest importers, most specifically of opium from Hong Kong and the subsequent distribution into North America. Until 1865, the opium trade was legal and unregulated, but after that the legislature issued licences and levied duties on its import and sale. By 1908, the opium trade was completely banned.

However, with the completion of the Canadian Pacific Railway terminus on Burrard Inlet on the mainland in 1886, Victoria lost some of its importance as the commercial centre of BC; that honour reverted to Vancouver. As a result, Victoria became known as a laid-back and gentle city in a beautiful, natural setting. Visitors to the city, such as Rudyard Kipling who wrote about Victoria, helped to cultivate and promote this image. In addition, the opening of the now world-renowned Butchart Gardens in 1904 firmly established Victoria on the world map of places to visit.

Following World War One, a real estate building boom took place in the city and many buildings erected during that period have contributed to the elegant flavour of Victoria. In the first years of the century, a number of municipalities surrounding the city were also incorporated: Saanich and Oak Bay in 1906, the Township of Esquimalt in 1912, with others to follow on the Saanich Peninsula.

Today, the city boasts two famous landmarks buildings: the British Columbia Parliament Buildings, completed in 1897 and home of the Legislative Assembly of British Columbia; and the equally eminent Fairmont Empress Hotel, which opened in 1908. A great number of Victoria's most renowned heritage homes were also built between 1912 and 1918.

In 1991, the year Michael Dunahee disappeared, Bill Vander Zalm was the Premier of British Columbia, followed in quick succession by Rita Johnson and Michael Harcourt all in that same year. British Columbia's Lieutenant Governor was David Lam. In the bigger picture, Canada's Prime Minister was Brian Mulroney and Ray Hnatyshyn was Governor General.

At the beginning of January that year the country was adjusting to (and complaining about) the recently introduced Goods and Services Tax (GST) and, at the same time, the Gulf War was raging in Iraq.

For Victoria, however, these events paled in comparison to the disappearance of Michael Wayne Dunahee in March, a few weeks before his fifth birthday. Michael became everyone's child that day and his disappearance permanently altered the way parents everywhere guarded the safety of their children.

What happened to him on that March morning in a playground area on the outskirts of the city? There was no crime scene to work from, no factual evidence, no witnesses to abduction. There are still no answers to that puzzle, which continues to haunt police investigators. All that was left was a mystery—an innocent child who completely vanished, leaving the authorities, and most especially his family, with a lifetime of unanswered questions.

For Michael's family, the day he disappeared was the day when their "perfect Eden" in Victoria turned into a living hell.

Blanshard
Elementary School

CHAPTER 1

Sunday, March 24, 1991

Call the police—I can't find my son.

—Bruce Dunahee, approximately 1:00 p.m. 24.3.91

The day started like any ordinary Sunday in the Dunahee household. Crystal Dunahee woke early to take care of her six-month-old daughter Caitlin and prepare breakfast for husband Bruce and son Michael in their two-bedroom unit in the Pioneer Co-Operative Housing Complex in Victoria West. Crystal was thinking about the exciting possibility of soon moving into a larger unit in the housing complex. Now with two children they needed a third bedroom, and their name was high on the list for a move that could be imminent.

The Dunahees were working class people. At that time, Crystal worked for the Guardian Insurance Company and Bruce worked hard at any and all jobs, such as gutter installation and roofing and at the Esquimalt shipyards whenever he could get hired on there.

Just over a week earlier, on March 10, baby Caitlin had been christened at Our Lady Queen of Peace Catholic Church in Esquimalt, and Crystal particularly treasured the photograph taken at the ceremony of her two children: Michael, wearing his striped, blue shirt and little red bow tie, proudly holding his baby sister. It was also the last time they were able to have a family portrait taken of the four of them together.

That particular Sunday was to be the first game of the spring season for the women's touch football team (the Hellcats) on which

Crystal played, but her game was not due to start until one o'clock so it would be a leisurely morning for the family.

After breakfast of his favourite cereal, Michael asked if he could play with his best friend, Ben Alexa, who lived in a neighbouring unit in the complex. He and Ben were a year apart in age and were inseparable. They loved to play together whenever they could. Crystal agreed, little knowing it would be the last time the two boys would ever play together.

Shortly after noon, the family loaded the car and set off for the Blanshard Elementary School playing field on Blanshard and King Streets, a rougher neighbourhood of Victoria. En route they made a slight detour to pick up Crystal's friend, Donna, a teammate on the touch football team. Michael was dressed in his favourite psychedelic-coloured rugby pants that Crystal had made for him, and was wearing his Mutant Ninja Turtle t-shirt under his blue hooded parka with red lining and elastic wrist bands.

Throughout her life, Crystal occasionally had "bad feelings" about things for no apparent reason; not exactly a premonition that something might happen, but simply uneasiness. Often, after one of these feelings, something unpleasant happened. She later recalled that as they drove to the field that morning she felt a bit anxious, but she dismissed it as nothing.

En route Michael asked if he might play at the playground when they got there. A play area with swings and slides was situated alongside the car park area and within 100 meters of the school playing field. Crystal did not immediately give her permission, but as they neared the parking area she agreed that he could play on the swings—but only if he stayed within sight. Both his parents told him that on no account must he wander away from the play area. Michael was an obedient little boy who listened to instructions and would not have defied his parents. He felt proud and important to be allowed this new independence of playing on his own for the first time.

The family pulled into the car park at approximately 12:35 p.m. and began unloading their car. It was a windy morning and Crystal pulled up Michael's hood to protect her son from the cold. Bruce and Crystal then began unloading her sporting equipment. Crystal bent down to put on her cleats and then placed Caitlin in her buggy in readiness for Bruce to walk her over to the playing field to watch Crystal's game. Two other games were already in progress on the field.

Michael had run off happily towards the playground area. Crystal remembers noticing two other children already playing there on the swings. They looked about Michael's age or perhaps a year or two older.

Between the time this was happening and when Bruce stood up on the rocky outcropping alongside the field to look back and check on Michael, approximately one minute elapsed—and Michael had disappeared from sight.

Bruce called out to him but there was no reply. Leaving the buggy with Crystal, he ran across the car park area to the playground where Michael should be, but there was no sign of him. He called again even louder.

"Michael! Michael! Where are you?"

No reply. Bruce began to feel panic, mixed first with annoyance that his son had perhaps disobeyed and wandered away. However, he knew that Michael was not a child who would have done that. Within seconds he was racing everywhere shouting Michael's name, attracting the attention of everyone in the vicinity. The games already in progress on the field stopped play and people began to run across to Crystal wondering what the commotion was all about. Within seconds, about twenty to thirty people were assisting in the search, running in all directions calling Michael's name—but all to no avail.

A man in a nearby house was cutting his grass, probably for the first time that year. Bruce called out to him.

"Call the police!" he shouted. "I can't find my son." This, of course, was long before the era of the cell phone.

That lost child call came into the Victoria police headquarters at approximately six minutes past one o'clock and Car 22 (officer on watch four) was dispatched to the scene. Back-up cars were also dispatched. In less than five minutes the police were on the scene and taking statements from Bruce and Crystal. They offered all the information they could, giving a clear description of their son and what he was wearing.

"Yes, he was dressed in his blue parka and brightly coloured rugby pants. Yes, he has blond hair and blue eyes. Yes, he is approximately three feet tall and weighs fifty-one pounds. He is beginning to show freckles on his nose.

Please just find him! Please..." the Dunahees begged.

Other officers searched between parked cars, outside nearby

houses and gardens, and continued door-to-door. Less than an hour had elapsed since the Dunahees first arrived at the car park, but to Bruce and Crystal it seemed like an eternity. Their son had simply vanished into thin air and no one had seen it happen. How could such a thing have occurred without anyone having witnessed it?

Between 1:37 and 1:42 p.m., three radio stations in Victoria (CFAX, CKDA and CJVI) were all notified about a "lost child," and the local CHEK TV station was given a picture of Michael for their 5:30 p.m. newscast.

Had Michael in fact ever reached the playground? Had his disappearance occurred in one split second as he ran between the three rows of parked cars towards the play area? Had someone already been waiting in a parked vehicle planning to grab him? No one knew. The police explored every possibility as they continued their door-to-door investigation in the neighbourhood, assuming initially that Michael might simply have wandered away and become lost.

The school portable classrooms between the playground and the road were all searched, inside and out. Every car in the car park was noted. Someone vaguely remembered seeing a brown van parked there earlier, but this could not be positively confirmed and no one had thought to take a licence plate number. One witness (a ten-year-old child) thought she had seen a small boy of Michael's description getting into such a vehicle.

It soon became apparent that Michael had not simply wandered away. Someone had most probably taken him. The search, however, continued all afternoon, spreading further afield around the city and beyond with the assistance of numerous volunteers. A small boy was missing, possibly abducted by person or persons unknown, but nothing was known for sure. He was a good little walker, so if he had indeed wandered away, it was thought he might even have made his way back towards the Esquimalt area where his grandmother, Barbara Dunahee, lived.

Within hours, British Columbia Ferries was alerted to Michael's disappearance, and a picture of him was faxed to ferries' staff the morning of March 25. Flyers were soon being handed out to ferry passengers on the Swartz Bay to Tsawwassen route to the mainland. The media was buzzing with the news.

At approximately six o'clock that evening, a "Michael Dunahee Command Centre" was set up at the Blanshard Community Police

Station across from the school, and that was where Bruce and Crystal anxiously waited for news. Other members of their family soon joined them.

The Dunahees were convinced that Michael would be found soon. He must have just wandered away and become lost; they were certain this was the case. They refused to believe someone had taken him. Who could possibly be so evil as to steal a little boy? Even if that were the case, they were positive that the police would quickly apprehend the perpetrator of this crime and Michael would be safely brought back to them. How could it be otherwise? This was Victoria, a safe city where evil, malicious things simply did not happen.

Eventually Crystal was persuaded to go home with Caitlin and wait there. Neighbours and friends informed her that her telephone was ringing off the hook, so maybe there was news from someone who knew what had happened to Michael. In an overwhelming daze, she arrived home to find that most of the calls were either from the media or from concerned friends who had heard the news being aired on the radio and on television.

She remembered little of the rest of the day. Her head was spinning with questions. Michael had never before been allowed to go off on his own, but on that particular day they had given him that privilege as a step toward maturity. Now Crystal asked herself why on earth they had let him do so on that particular day. Why hadn't she insisted he stay beside his dad? Why? Why? Her mind was full of "whys" and "what ifs." Most of all, she wondered, why hadn't she trusted her uneasy feeling that morning?

At some point she supposed that she must have fallen into a fitful sleep, praying she would wake up the next morning to find it had all been some horrible dream and they would find Michael in his bed in the room he shared with his baby sister.

But the next day the shocking truth was still there. There was no good news. The reality was unchanged—Michael had gone. Their ordinary Sunday had turned into a ghastly nightmare—and this was just the beginning.

Life for the Dunahees would never again be the same.

CHAPTER 2

The First Two Months

A connection or two away from the truth...
—Victoria Police Officer

According to Child Find Canada, all missing children cases can be divided into three main categories: runaways, stranger abductions, or parental abductions.

Runaways usually comprise 49 percent of missing children, and in most instances these are older children who are trying to escape from what they believe to be unsolvable problems at home, most specifically abusive situations that might be physical, sexual or emotional. In the case of Michael Dunahee, it was soon obvious that he had not run away from his parents.

Stranger abduction, although given the highest profile in the media because of the often-monstrous nature of the crime, comprises only 2 percent of missing children cases.

The remaining 49 percent of missing children cases involve parental abductions, often the result of a marriage break-up and an ongoing bitter child custody battle between the parents. Parental abduction cases are initially the hardest for the police to deal with because they must thoroughly investigate the backgrounds of both parents of the missing child and determine whether one or the other has instigated the abduction as a calculated act of vengeance against the other.

It was, therefore, inevitable that the Victoria police had to first eliminate Crystal and Bruce Dunahee as suspects in Michael's disappearance. This is a particularly painful process for both the police and the parents, especially when the parents appear to love their child and are desperately worried about him.

Within seconds, the Dunahees had been struck by lightning that day—their little boy was gone. But to enable the police to carry out their investigation thoroughly, Bruce and Crystal also had to undergo in-depth interviews; it was a necessary evil. Even the bizarre possibility that he might never even have been brought to the area by his parents that day had to be explored.

The current state of Bruce and Crystal's marriage was examined and many questions into their backgrounds were posed. Fathers are invariably the first suspects in any child abduction case. When Bruce initially became the number one suspect, he was asked to take a lie detector (polygraph) test, to which he readily agreed.

Throughout these interviews, it was determined that both Bruce and Crystal's lives had for the most part been grounded in the Esquimalt area.

Crystal was born in 1961 to a very young mother who was forced to give her up for adoption. Her adoptive parents, Helen Mary Caldewell and Jeff Jeffries, raised her as their daughter along with an older brother (also adopted) and three of their own birth children, so Crystal Jeffries became the middle child of five siblings: Bruce, Art, Larry and Dorothy. She attended Rock Heights and Lampson Elementary Schools and later Esquimalt High School, after which she went to Camosun College where she took courses in business administration. Later she worked for the Guardian Insurance Company and had steadily climbed the ladder with that company where, over a period of sixteen years, she rose from the typing pool to the claims adjustment department.

Bruce was also an Esquimalt boy. Born in September 1961 to Harvey and Barbara Dunahee, he was raised with older brother Keith and younger sister Karen in a Catholic household. After the birth of Keith in Victoria in 1960, the Dunahees moved to Fort Francis, Ontario, where Bruce and Karen were born. Harvey served in the navy before joining the Coast Guard and moving back to Esquimalt in 1965. For much of Bruce's early years, his father was at sea. Harvey was a tough man who liked his drink and ran a "tight ship" at home. He was strict with all his children and always made them tow the line. His wife might well have been the peacemaker in the home. Although Bruce and his brother liked to argue, they were also the best of friends. They were altar boys at church and basically enjoyed a traditional family life with the requisite Sunday dinners together and family time. The Dunahees were essentially an average, close-knit family who cared about one another.

In his youth, Bruce had run with a thrill-seeking group of Esquimalt boys who were often rowdy and liked to drink and party, but they never got into any really serious trouble.

Bruce also attended Esquimalt High School and knew Crystal, but did not "officially" meet her until they had both left school. They met again in May 1983 at a bowling alley when Bruce offered to spare for the team on which Crystal was playing. They started dating, even though Crystal maintained they were complete opposites in many ways. Bruce had the "bad boy" image; Crystal was the "good girl" who would spend her Friday nights bowling with friends while Bruce might have been out partying. However, on October 8, five months after that meeting in the bowling alley, they were married. Three years later, on May 12, 1986 at 11:05 a.m., their son Michael came into the world, with Caitlin arriving on September 7, 1990.

By March 1991, the Dunahees were, in essence, a typical young, hard working couple with two children. At the time of Michael's abduction, Bruce and Crystal were not estranged and there was definitely no question of any dispute over the custody of Michael. In addition, there appeared to be no one in their circle of friends who would wish to harm their son or punish them by taking him. The police could find no skeletons in the Dunahee closet, and they determined that Bruce and Crystal had done absolutely nothing wrong the day of Michael's disappearance.

First dead end.

Family members, friends and neighbours were interviewed also. Everyone became a suspect until proven otherwise. Bruce's brother, Keith, had been hiking up at Cape Scott on the tip of Vancouver Island that weekend and the RCMP posted a notice on the trail for him to contact the police immediately when he came out of the bush. Bruce's sister, Karen, had been at work that day and did not hear the news about her little nephew until she got home around five o'clock. She was devastated, as was everyone in both the Dunahee and Jeffries families.

Crystal's mother telephoned her other daughter, Dorothy Arsenault, living in Ottawa at the time with her husband Chris who was serving in the military. When the phone rang at 5:00 a.m. on the morning of March 25 Dorothy assumed it was a call for her husband and something to do with his work. He took the call, but when he came back into the bedroom to wake her he was trying not to cry as he told her about Michael's disappearance. Dorothy thought it could not possibly be true. They switched on TV to hear the latest news and then Dorothy telephoned her mother back. She learned that Crystal had not wanted to tell her immediately because Dorothy was three months pregnant with her first child, and Crystal, ever concerned about others, especially her little sister, did not want this news to upset her and cause her problems with her pregnancy.

However, as time went by, Dorothy became increasingly stressed because of the distance between her and her sister with whom she had always been close. She wanted to be with Crystal to help in whatever way she could. Eventually both her husband and her doctor agreed it would be safe for her to fly to Victoria and would cause her less stress than being 4,800 kilometers (3,000 miles) away in Ontario fretting about the situation. Upon her arrival a few days later, the sisters hugged and Dorothy held her little niece, Caitlin, in her arms for the first time. It was an emotional moment.

Crystal and Bruce were back at the Blanshard Community Police Command Centre early on the Monday morning, March 25, anxiously waiting for news. Things were moving quickly in the investigation, with over 100 officers designated to Michael's disappearance. The *Victoria Times-Colonist* headline that morning read: POLICE FEAR BOY, 4, ABDUCTED

The city of Victoria ground to a standstill and an entire community came together to assist in the search. City work crews, garbage men, and ordinary people on the street were all helping, pounding the pavement and looking inside dumpsters and discarded fridges in backyards.

Posters were soon printed and distributed by volunteers throughout the capital region and beyond. Over thirty-five cities across Canada were soon aware of Michael's disappearance and the news also spread fast throughout the United States.

Within the first twenty-four hours of Michael's disappearance, the Federal Bureau of Investigation (FBI) Behavioral Sciences Unit

(BSU) was contacted for their input and assistance. A few weeks later, on May 5, police officers from Victoria headed down to Virginia in the States to consult in person with the unit. The BSU, which was established in 1972, is one of the instructional components of the FBI's Training Division at Quantico, Virginia, and its mission is to develop and provide numerous training and research programs to enhance the FBI's administration and understanding of violent crimes.

The BSU quickly drew up a profile on the Dunahee case, which suggested that the abductor(s) might well have been someone familiar with the area and perhaps had even lived close by. At the very least, they surmised that it would have to have been someone who knew the various street patterns around Blanshard Street, as some of those streets were one-way and it would not have been easy to make a quick get-away without knowing the area well. You would have to know which streets to take if you were leaving in a hurry.

On the other hand, if the abductor was someone who lived close by, Michael might well have been grabbed and then hidden nearby for some time before being taken further away. The abductor would most probably have had the appearance of an ordinary person, blending in with others in the area. He might have been dressed in sweat pants, like many others arriving in the area to participate in or to watch the sporting events on the adjoining field. There would most likely have been nothing out of the ordinary about his or her demeanor that would have attracted attention.

According to the BSU, there are usually four motives for child abduction: ransom; substitution of the child for another; pedophilia; or the sale of the child.

In the Michael Dunahee case, the motive of ransom was initially ruled out. Later, however, in November 1992, there was one ransom call made to the Dunahees. At that time, someone contacted Bruce and told him to deliver $10,000 to a specific location at a Vancouver park and then Michael would be returned. Bruce would have followed through with the instructions, in full co-operation with the police, but the person never called back with further directions. It was just one more crank call.

Substitution of a child was initially also ruled out because of lack of evidence, but nothing has ever been proven either way. The police also investigated sexual predators they had on file who might fit the profile and could possibly have been in the neighbourhood at that particular time. They also exhausted all possible avenues concerning the sale of a child; the last recorded case of selling a child in North America had occurred in March of 1989. Nothing seemed to click or come together.

Michael's disappearance was soon profiled on the TV show *America's Most Wanted*. Michael's case became so high profile on the show that it was featured an unprecedented five times over the coming weeks.

John Walsh, the host of *AMW*, knew well the horror of a missing child, having had his own six-year-old son, Adam, abducted ten years earlier in 1981. Adam was taken from the toy department of a Sears department store at the Hollywood Mall, within sight of the Hollywood police station. Tragically, Adam was later found murdered. For years, the prime suspect in Adam's murder was serial killer, Ottis Toole. Finally, in 2008, on his deathbed, he admitted to his psychologist that he had indeed murdered Adam.

In addition to being the host of *AMW*, Walsh remains a strong advocate for anti-crime and human rights. He is also part owner of the Museum of Crime & Punishment in Washington, DC.

Meanwhile Crystal and Bruce Dunahee were feeling completely helpless.

"There is nothing I can physically do to find him even though it is my son who is missing," Bruce said in an interview. "You do everything you can to protect your children and then something like this happens. Why?" Bruce Dunahee was a completely broken man, feeling inadequate and distraught about the fact that he had not been able to protect his son.

Crystal knew she had to remain strong for their six-month-old daughter, but how, she wondered, would she ever be able to go on? How would she learn to continue with normal everyday activities again when her mind was in a swirl of fear and worry? Would she ever be able to smile or laugh again until Michael was back home where he belonged? It helped to have her family close and her younger sister in town.

The day after Michael's disappearance, the police had worked on a complete re-enactment of that Sunday morning in the car park and all areas adjacent to the Blanshard Elementary School. They asked everyone involved in the football games and all those who had parked there to return to the exact spot they were in that Sunday morning. Each person was then interviewed, but no one could recall seeing anything amiss.

The one person who had vaguely remembered seeing a dark-coloured van (possibly brown) also thought that it had disappeared by the time the search for Michael began. No one had any memory of when the van might have arrived or left the car park. The van and its driver had not returned for the re-enactment. That vehicle (a van, camper or pick-up) became the police's first strong lead in the investigation, but within a short time, this too led nowhere.

That was when one of the most heinous chapters of the investigation occurred. During that first week, five telephone calls were made to the Dunahee household and were recorded on their answering machine. Each time the person repeated the same contemptible message:

> Voice: "He's been murdered! We've murdered him."
> Crystal: "Who's we?"
> Voice: "A sacrifice to the devil."
> Crystal: "Who *are* you?"
> Voice: "We murdered him. You're not going to get Michael back."
> Crystal: "Who *are* you?"
> Voice: "You can't have him back. We murdered him. Hare Krishna. Hare Krishna. Hare Krishna!"

The message ended there. At the time, the police did not release the actual recorded voice of the caller to the public because of their ongoing investigation into this person who was believed to be an adult drifter with no apparent connection to any religion.

The Hare Krishna mantra at the end of the message had no bearing on a satanic cult, but there were also those people who believed in satanic cults and thought that Michael had been abducted by one. It was suggested that it was no coincidence that he was taken on Palm Sunday, seven days before Easter and seven streets away from Easter Street.

These believers also thought that Michael's disappearance was connected to a so-called "true life" book called *Michelle Remembers* by Dr. Joseph Pazdor. In the book, a young girl, Michelle, claimed that her own mother had offered her to a satanic cult in Victoria,

British Columbia (supposedly thought to be the satanic cult capital of the world, second only to Geneva in Switzerland) as a personal sacrifice to be prepared for the "Feast of the Beast." Meanwhile she was kept in a dirt cage and tortured. Eventually she was considered "unworthy" so was returned to her mother who was told to only come back to them when she could bring them a dutiful son.

The book was mostly sensational in context and may well have been pure fiction. Victoria had certainly never been considered a city where satanic cults ran riot or were even known to exist. Nonetheless, some people still thought there was some sort of connection between the names Michael and Michelle, and also the fact that the name Michael is the name of the archangel who threw Satan out of heaven.

Initially, the police refused to comment on all of this or the loathsome messages left on the Dunahees' answering machine, as they were still continuing their investigation into tracing the caller. Every lead had to be followed, even the most bizarre, such as the possible existence of a satanic cult that might have taken Michael.

However, whenever a disappearance of a child occurs, there are always disturbed people who wish to sensationalize the event, oblivious to the pain they are adding to an already distraught family. Eventually, the cult theory and the unsettling calls were dismissed as being the work of an unstable person, against whom charges were being considered. Nonetheless, all theories had to be considered in an investigation such as this one. Ultimately nothing was proven and the lead fizzled out.

But the tips and leads kept coming. In the first two months of Michael's disappearance, over 200 US sightings were reported that needed to be looked into, some in Georgia, California and New Jersey. *America's Most Wanted* continued running the case, and following each show there was a flood of new tips to be followed up. The distribution of a half million posters far and wide and Michael's photograph portrayed on the side and rear of buses were all bringing in more sightings, and the police in Victoria were working around the clock, diligently following up on every single lead.

Crystal's stepbrother, serving in the military in Germany, spread posters in Europe, and posters also reached New Zealand and beyond. Michael's angelic little face was soon known worldwide.

Eventually, as the investigation grew beyond all proportions, the

Command Centre had to move from the Blanshard Street Community Centre. Even the telephone lines had crashed due to overload. A basement room at the Canadian Legion Hall in Esquimalt was donated for a new Command Centre, and from there volunteers and the Organized Labour Council gave hours of their time, printing more fliers and posters and assisting in the search.

Steve Orcherton, at that time spokesperson and secretary treasurer of the Victoria Labour Council, came forward to offer his assistance. His own son was the same age as Michael and he felt a strong empathy with the family. He knew by then that the Dunahee search team needed office supplies, equipment and postage, so Orcherton approached the local unions and asked for their support in supplying these items, which he then delivered to the search centre.

The offices of Child Find BC became involved and offered their services to the Dunahee family and to the police investigation.

Reward money of $10,000 had been donated and then was doubled by Vancouver stock promoter and one-time owner of the BC Lions football team, Murray Pezim.

The prime minister's wife, Mila Mulroney, made a special announcement vowing that she would do everything in her power to help the police find Michael.

Detective John Smith, who was coordinating the Dunahee case in Victoria, strongly believed they were now just "a connection or two away from the truth." When asked by a reporter if he had made that statement out of faith or logic, he replied "both." He and all members of the Victoria police assumed that Michael was still alive somewhere and would soon be found, simply because they had found no evidence which would prove otherwise.

Bruce and Crystal were comforted by the knowledge that they were being helped by so many people locally and across the country, and that the police still held positive thoughts. No one was giving up.

But time moved on with no results. March turned into April, and April became May, and suddenly it was just a few days before what would have been Michael's fifth birthday—May 12, 1991.

Crystal and Bruce firmly believed that their son would be returned to them before that date. It simply had to happen. They knew he would not be the same little boy, because whatever had happened to him in the interim, he must, one way or the other, have gone through a traumatic experience; but they were convinced they could help him through whatever might have occurred and that he would once again be the same happy, innocent child who had run off to play that morning.

They kept his bedroom just as it was before he left on that fateful Sunday morning. Crystal even purchased his favourite toy as a birthday gift for him—a Nintendo set. She had wrapped it with care. It now lay waiting for him on his bed.

CHAPTER 3

The Initial Leads

If I didn't have Caitlin to look after, I don't know what I would do...

—Crystal Dunahee

Michael's fifth birthday came and went.

More leads kept coming in, but nothing was panning out. In the beginning, Crystal and Bruce got their hopes up each time the police told them of a new development that might be the one clue needed to find their son. Every time their phone rang their hearts skipped a beat. This could be it! Michael had been found and would be coming home to them. Each time a police car drove by their home, they prayed it would stop at their door and Michael would be inside.

They were living a life of incredible highs and staggering lows and it soon had a damaging effect on them both; the stress on their marriage became apparent. Crystal admitted that she and Bruce had many "blow-ups" and arguments in those early months. Bruce once went and sat in a hotel room for three days, in his shorts, watching TV and drinking beer. Crystal also went away to her father's house on one occasion and stayed for two weeks, "just to try and get focused." It was simply how they both initially worked through the agony of losing Michael. There was no easy way to get through those early days.

Incidents such as these fuelled the rumours that started floating around town of their separation and possible divorce; but with the help of grief counselling meetings, which they started in June of 1991 and attended twice a month, they were able to go on one day at a time. In fact, over the years, rumours occasionally spread that the Dunahees had divorced. Many couples would have given up on both their marriage and of ever finding Michael, but not Bruce and Crystal. On the contrary—despite the fear, the stress and the unending sadness, they were kept together by their shared bond of love for their son. Ultimately, that bond made their marriage stronger.

A week into the search, Bruce had slept only twenty hours and he spent most of his waking hours at the Command Centre. Most nights he stayed there until midnight, working relentlessly to find ways of getting his son back home. When Father's Day came around that year, Bruce had a complete meltdown and took out his anger and frustration by kicking the nearest pole.

"I was pissed off at everything," he said later, "a lack of progress in the search mostly. But, I quickly learned my lesson from that display of anger. I broke my left foot!"

They were always hoping for the best, but at the same time, expecting the worse. Where was their son? How could a child completely disappear? It made no sense. Days turned into weeks, weeks into months.

"They say time heals all wounds," Bruce said, "but basically I believe that's a load of crap." This was one wound that would not heal.

Crystal tried her best to carry on a normal life with Caitlin. Having her daughter to take care of kept her sane. She took Caitlin for walks, pushing her buggy, automatically looking back expecting to see Michael trotting along behind them. She watched other children playing together in parks or playgrounds and wondered where her son was.

"Michael should be there, playing with them," she told a reporter on one occasion. "If I didn't have Caitlin to look after I don't know what I would do."

During the first month of Michael's disappearance, twenty-hour days had been the norm for the Victoria Police department, during which they investigated every tip or sighting that came in. It was a monumental task.

Michael had supposedly been spotted at a highway rest stop in New York; at a convenience store in New Jersey; and in a home video filmed on northern Vancouver Island. Someone even called to say that Michael was living in the United States and had his skin dyed black. Each of these leads was thoroughly checked out. Each went nowhere.

The first strong lead had, of course, been the brown van supposedly seen at the location from which Michael disappeared. It was a ten-year-old girl who had spotted the van, inside of which she claimed to have seen a tan-coloured dog in a cage. She described a cargo-type sliding side door on the van, which also had a rear door with a tinted window. She believed she had seen a boy matching Michael's description entering the van, and she had even drawn a picture of how she remembered the van.

While this lead was being thoroughly investigated, another disturbing incident occurred up-island in the town of Duncan. On Tuesday, March 27 a one-year-old First Nations boy went missing from a shopping mall. Although there appeared to be no connection to Michael's disappearance, police nonetheless had to investigate every possibility, and certainly a second apparent abduction sent panic into the hearts of parents all over Vancouver Island. However, the child was soon found, cold and hungry, near the Cowichan River, and his mother was later charged with neglect and public mischief for reporting him as having been taken.

By March 28, with the FBI involved and police heading up-island to look into other leads on Michael's case, things became more and more perplexing. A list of current prison inmates and known sex offenders out on parole was compiled and these people were all interviewed and investigated. The Dunahees insisted that Michael was a street-smart little boy and had been told how to react if a stranger approached him. They felt sure he would not willingly have gone off with anyone.

At that point, the van still remained the strongest lead, but there were known to be 20,000 brown vans in BC at that time and about 6,000 in Greater Victoria alone. There were also many conflicting statements being made about the van, and whether the sighting had happened much earlier in the morning, before the Dunahees had even arrived at the park.

The second strong lead came from witnesses who claimed to have seen a man "hanging around the area near the park at Kings Road and Wark Streets."

On March 30, the police released a composite drawing of this person. He was not considered a suspect, just a person of interest they wanted to interview as a possible witness. He was described as a short, thirty- to forty-year-old man with a large nose and whiteish-grey hair that was thin on top. He was wearing grey rugby-style pants and a blue jacket with a white stripe around the middle.

As a result of the drawing, the police interviewed five look-alikes who all matched the description but, once again, this lead came to nothing.

By the end of March, even psychics were getting involved in the search for Michael, offering their own interpretations of the events. One Victoria psychic, Lady Zee, plus a clairvoyant and another un-named psychic, were all working together at the site of Michael's disappearance. They all believed he was still alive somewhere and that his abduction was unlikely to be random. They stated there was "more of a story to it than that," and thought it had been strategically planned ahead. Michael was not just any child who had been taken indiscriminately. Perhaps the person or people who took him were specifically looking for a four-year-old boy with blond hair and blue eyes. He had been watched before he was taken and it was possible, they stated, that he might have known one of the abductors.

Famous US psychic, Jean Kozocari, agreed that the abduction was not random, but she was not sure about the brown van connection; and although she had strong feelings in general about the case, she would not work on it unless called in by the family or the police. She stated that most psychics just get odd flashes of information and sometimes these flashes don't make any sense because they are difficult to interpret. It is rather like a jigsaw puzzle that needs all the pieces in place before the complete picture becomes clear. In other words, it was exactly the same scenario as the police had been experiencing. And the jigsaw pieces were simply not coming together, as one tip after another led nowhere. Any information coming from psychics also went nowhere and caused even more frustration.

Then, on April 1, the police announced their investigation was changing direction. They had in their possession some photographs taken at the playground, which showed another child who resembled Michael. That child's mother had come forward and identified him as her son. The photographs showing the other child had been taken long before Michael Dunahee and his parents arrived at the park, and this cleared up some discrepancies concerning the brown van. Possibly the ten-year-old girl witnessed this other child getting into a van and not Michael at all.

On April 9, there was a strong break in the case when there were two apparent sightings of Michael in New Jersey. The media played up this news and suddenly there was new life being breathed into Michael's case.

Reports out of Maple Shade, New Jersey, a small town with a population of 25,000 people situated ten kilometres (six miles) east of Philadelphia, stated that a man had apparently been approached by a small boy resembling Michael who told him he was looking for his "mommy and daddy." The witness, a New Jersey resident, said he could not fully understand the boy at the time, as he appeared to have what he described as an English accent, although it could possibly have been Canadian; but the witness stated he was tone-deaf in one ear and the boy was talking to him on that side of his face. He was sure, however, that the boy had said, "I am from Vancouver and I'm looking for my mommy and daddy."

A second New Jersey sighting of Michael had also been reported from a woman who said she was 50 percent certain that she had seen a child bearing a strong resemblance to Michael Dunahee in "suspicious circumstances" inside a black truck on April 2.

The New Jersey sightings both resulted from a showing of *America's Most Wanted* on April 5 and they offered what the Victoria police at first described as a "glimmer of hope" in the case, but they warned the Dunahees to remain cautiously optimistic. Bruce was ready to head down to New Jersey as soon as the police requested him to do so.

Unfortunately, the New Jersey witness's story seemed to become more embellished with details as time went by. Some of the details he described were also changing, especially after he had seen the next episode of *America's Most Wanted*. Although he still remained 100 percent positive of what he had seen on April 4, he admitted his memory had only been sparked *after* he saw the episode on April 5. He wished he had seen the earlier episode and then, when the incident in the store had occurred, he would have studied the boy's face more.

"But I am sure this is the same child and he is alive," he said. "I'm just sorry I didn't understand him more clearly or take seriously what he said to me. If I had seen that episode the night before, I would have been sure it was him."

The incident in question had supposedly taken place at 3:00 p.m. at the Cumberland Farms Convenience Store where the man was standing in line and talking with other customers in the store about the terrific heat wave they were experiencing that week. He said that suddenly a little boy had approached him and said his name was Michael followed by another word beginning with "D" which he did not hear clearly. The boy was wearing a white t-shirt with red writing on it and had on long blue pants.

Apparently the child then said, "I am trying to get back to my mommy and daddy. Please help me."

Assuming that the boy had strayed from his parents and possibly had come from a nearby housing complex, the witness replied, "Okay, if your parents don't come in shortly, we'll call the police."

At that moment, a little girl with olive-coloured skin and dark hair called from the door of the store, "Come on Michael. It's time to go."

The man supposedly then asked the boy, "Is that your sister?" and the boy replied, "No."

"Are you with those people?" and the boy said, "Yes."

The witness then claimed that a black man dressed in a dark suit and white knit shirt called to the children from the door, "Come on kids, it's time to go."

They then both got into the back seat of a large 1970s model car. When asked, the witness said he had not noticed any suitcases or baggage in the car, and the boy did not appear to be upset but, thinking about it later, he said the boy might have been on some kind of tranquilizer. He also said he had expected to see a white woman in the car as it was not unusual to see a couple of mixed race with white or black children.

The next night while watching *America's Most Wanted* he had said to himself, "Oh my God, I've seen that child before. I was shocked."

He immediately notified the authorities, but claimed they had not taken his sighting seriously at first, so he also decided to contact the number given for the Victoria police, a place in Canada he had never even heard of before. He remembered the boy mentioning a place beginning with "V" which could have been Vancouver or Victoria.

The only trouble with this very promising sighting was the fact that the "witness" seemed to add to and change his story as he went along, and the new details seemed to be enhanced only *after* he heard the complete story of Michael's disappearance. He also included in his story the appearance of a "black man" after having heard that the original woman's sighting nearby had mentioned that the boy was with a black man.

So, by April 16, the police, both in Victoria and in New Jersey, were becoming somewhat sceptical. The New Jersey police continued to investigate the story and reported that the convenience store manager remembered speaking with a man, but had no recollection of ever seeing a little boy talking to him.

After having heard of the reward money being offered for information, had this witness simply exaggerated his story? Had he in fact ever seen a boy at all?

Nonetheless, the police continued to investigate the sighting thoroughly, but by then it was just being treated as one of more than 1,600 tips they had received from the airing of the five showings on *America's Most Wanted.*

The police later admitted that, by contrast, one of the most promising tips they ever received and the one they became the most excited about came from an Idaho preschool which, like many schools across the US at that time, was displaying the missing poster of Michael Dunahee on their walls. Apparently a couple from Arizona had dropped off a small boy at the school and then hastily left, saying they would be back in a week to pick him up. The boy came inside, looked up at the poster and immediately said, "That's me!"

Sadly, investigation into this very promising lead also showed it to be false.

Soon after that, a blue jacket resembling Michael's was found in Kaslo, BC, but proved not to be his. And a boy in Albany, New York, who was reported to have a strong resemblance to Michael, was given a blood test to prove his identity, but again it was established he was not Michael.

By the time the first anniversary of Michael's disappearance came around, Don Bland, a Victoria detective sergeant then working the Dunahee case, stated that his department had investigated thousands of tips and 789 possible sightings.

There would be many more leads in the years ahead, some

which raised the hopes of the Dunahee family, only to bring them crashing down once again. Their roller coaster of emotions would continue month after month, year after year, and still answers were not found.

Nonetheless, even twenty-one years later, the police still maintain that just one small piece of information could well lead them back to any one of those initial tips and be the missing piece of the jigsaw puzzle, which would be the answer needed to solve the mystery.

CHAPTER 4

Keeping the Hope Alive

**I'll keep on for as long as it takes...
I know my son is still alive.**

—Bruce Dunahee

As time went by, it became increasingly difficult for everyone to stay optimistic. Nonetheless, during those first weeks and months after Michael disappeared, the community of Victoria rallied around the Dunahee family, with hundreds of volunteers going above and beyond to try and find answers to the mystery.

By Sunday, March 31 the reward fund for information had risen to $40,000. Michael's granddad, Harvey Dunahee, had already organized and led a volunteer ground search effort with Metchosin Search & Rescue at Goldstream Park. At the Gordon Head Recreation Centre near Victoria, a family-type, no-alcohol dance for all ages was organized for Saturday, April 6, with all proceeds going to the Dunahee Family Search Fund. Members of the Hellcats, Crystal's touch football team, also organized fundraisers, and students as far away as St. Laurent, Quebec held a "dance-a-thon" to help raise funds for the Dunahees. Our Lady Queen of Peace Church in Esquimalt held frequent masses and candlelight vigils offering prayers for Michael's safe return.

While all this support certainly helped to sustain Bruce and Crystal through their many moments of utter despair, the one thing they most wanted—to see their son safely home again—was not happening.

Then, just before Christmas 1991, a lead came in to the Victoria Police Department from Albany, New York, stating that a small boy matching Michael's description was seen panhandling on the street there.

"Here I was on the phone for about two hours in the early hours of the morning trying to describe my son to the police officer in Albany who was sitting in front of the kid," said Bruce. It was a painful experience for Bruce, and heartbreaking when later a blood test revealed that this child wasn't Michael.

During those first days, Scott Johnson, a friend of the Dunahees who was visiting Victoria on a break from Eastern Washington University in Cheney where he was attending school, turned on his TV one night to watch the news and saw his old pal, Bruce, pleading for everyone to help find his son. Scott was dumbfounded.

Scott and Bruce had attended Esquimalt High School together and became close friends when they both played for a flag football team called the Esquimalt All Blues. Back in those days, Bruce had the nickname "Bruiser." He always played with reckless abandon and had no fear; even when taking a beating from the opposing team, he still played aggressively and well. They had played hard and partied even harder afterwards.

The men would frequent the local pubs to celebrate or drown their sorrows, depending on whether it had been a win or a loss. Later Scott remembered Bruce bringing Crystal along, and eventually he got to know her well.

Scott's memories included the many Sunday mornings when the team would meet up at someone's house for coffee, chatting and laughing as they got ready for the game.

"I also remember, like it was only yesterday, when Bruce and Crystal started to bring Michael with them," said Scott. "Michael was just learning to walk by then, and as we all sat around the kitchen table drinking coffee, we watched little Michael take some of his very first steps. From then on, Michael was seen at most of the men's games and at all the tournaments. He would also be hanging out with Bruce and Crystal while they worked at the concession. He was never far from their side, and seeing Michael at the games was as natural to me as seeing any one of our teammates there."

Once back at school, Scott thought long and hard for ways to help his old friends, and eventually he came up with the idea of organizing a charity run on the one-year anniversary of Michael's disappearance to help raise funds and keep up public awareness of Michael's case. Knowing that Crystal and Bruce were both athletic, the idea of a run seemed like a perfect way to bring in more money for the Dunahee Family Search Fund.

Scott realized that "after the dust settles from something like the Michael Dunahee disappearance, it is often replaced with other pressing issues of the moment." He did not want Michael's case to become just another nine-day-wonder.

He strongly believed that if he could make a lot of noise with this run it could become an annual fundraising event, which would increase awareness of the bigger picture and the most important goal, which was to tell the stories of all abducted children through Child Find Canada.

With this in mind, Scott met with Bruce and Crystal and put the idea to them. They readily agreed, and thus the first "Keep The Hope Alive Fun Run" was born.

That first five-kilometer run took place from the Cedar Hill Recreation Centre on Sunday, March 22, 1992. By this time Scott was doing an internship with the Saanich Parks and Recreation Department and Cedar Hill was his main workplace. He obtained permission from his supervisor to use the recreation centre, but the supervisor warned him that most first charity runs like the one he was proposing usually only attract about 100 participants. Scott was determined to prove that theory wrong. He knew the event would be an emotional one, but he felt sure that if he promoted it in the right way he could get a lot more than 100 people involved.

His plan of action was to first approach the *Victoria Times Colonist* newspaper, along with every other local newspaper; CHEK TV news; CFAX radio and the "Q" radio station; all in Victoria. The *Victoria Times Colonist* agreed to provide free advertising prior to the run, and wrote many stories before, during and after the event. All the local community newspapers also ran advertisements and stories about the run and Michael's disappearance.

With volunteer help, he made a mountain of posters and flyers advertising the event, all of which he plastered around town wherever he could find a suitable spot. A designer volunteered her time to design the posters and flyers, and Monk Office Supply in Victoria provided Scott with all the paper needed plus all the photocopying completely free. Everyone wanted to display the posters in their store windows or on their community notice boards or in their school newsletters. Scott soon had an army of volunteers who were willing to distribute the posters throughout the community. They even went door-to-door in the surrounding neighbourhood where the run was about to take place.

He also contacted many businesses, such as Shoppers Drug Mart and Mr. Grocers, and asked if they would like to sponsor the run for products and promotions. Everyone embraced the idea and registration for the run began almost immediately.

By then, Scott was a man on a mission. He talked to Parents Association Committees (PAC) and went to all the local schools, speaking directly with the kids during school assemblies. Once the word got out, the whole thing simply snowballed.

"I knew it was going to be big," said Scott, "but not quite as big as it got. The more it grew, the more newspapers and TV and radio stations wanted to talk to me in order to promote it. All the newspapers, television and radio advertisements were donated completely free that first year. As soon as those people were approached they simply said, 'How many times would you like your ad to run?' It was unbelievable support."

In many ways this was typical of the warmth and generosity of the Greater Victoria community.

Before long, more stories were run on BCTV (now Global) and the CBC, and they turned out on the day of the event. Scott also managed to obtain coverage across the country and soon people from all over Canada called him, wanting to help. It was an amazing and overwhelming outpouring of help and public exposure for a missing child.

One of Scott's strongest memories of people's willingness to help was that of Linden Soles, a local news anchor at that time. Scott had asked Soles if he would consider being the Master of Ceremonies for the event. He knew it was a long shot as Soles was a popular and busy man.

"I really sweet-talked him into it, and I think Bruce and Crystal had also talked with him...they were probably more instrumental in getting him than I was. However, he agreed to do the first run and, not only that, he came back yearly during the first few runs to continue being our emcee, even after he had landed a job with CNN in Atlanta. He was very much in demand at that time, but he still came back every year from Atlanta for as long as he was able, just to be involved."

The entry fee for the run was ten dollars for adults (and eight dollars for children) and included a t-shirt; or for two dollars less, people could enter the run and not receive a t-shirt. A friend of Scott's had a mobile t-shirt press business that he ran from a semi truck and trailer, which he would drive to large events and make the t-shirts on site. The t-shirts were a great success with everyone who entered the run, and people willingly paid the small entry fee to obtain one.

With the agreement of Bruce and Crystal, Scott also incorporated a dance in the weekend event—held on the Saturday evening before the run—which was well attended and brought in even more funding for the search effort.

Other volunteers also pitched in with their own fundraising efforts to support the run. Three canoeists—Henry Ravensdale, Gordon Oliphant and Arped Satory—left the Inner Harbour in Victoria in the early hours of March 22 and paddled for eighteen hours across to False Creek in Vancouver. They made the journey across in a two-man canoe escorted by a boat, and used a three-man rotation with two paddling all the time while the third rested in the boat. They arrived in False Creek at 4:25 the next morning, tired and sore, but delighted they had been able to raise more money for the search effort.

A Sooke school vice-principal, David Bennett, spearheaded another incredible effort. He wrote a pamphlet entitled *Child Abduction Prevention—Street-proofing and Strategies,* which was shipped to all members of the Canadian Association of Principals on the first anniversary of Michael's disappearance. He had first started working on the idea after participating in the original searches for Michael the previous March, and hoped it would soon become required reading for elementary school children across Canada.

On the actual anniversary of Michael's disappearance, Tuesday, March 24, 1992, students from Blanshard Elementary School walked to City Hall downtown to be greeted by Mayor David Turner, Crystal Dunahee and Detective Inspector Fred Mills. They then returned to the school to plant a tree in Michael's name, to be called "The Tree of Hope." The tree still stands on the grounds of the old elementary school, a symbol of hope against the despair of the tragedy that occurred there.

In contrast to all this support for the Dunahees, a negative aspect suddenly intruded on the scenario. Among the numerous articles written about the case, one in particular, published around the time of the first anniversary of Michael's disappearance, stood out from the others because of its callous viewpoint. It was a column, named, ironically, "Pleasants' Pen" in *The Esquimalt News*, a local community newspaper.

The piece was titled, "There Comes a Time to End the Search," and the writer expressed the opinion that after a whole year of fruitless searching, it might well be time to call a halt. The article asked why, after a year of experiencing numerous leads going nowhere and wasting many hours and a great deal of money, searchers would still continue their somewhat hopeless task of keeping alive the hope that Michael could be found. The article suggested that there simply must come a time to end the search. Everything had been done and now it should be over and the Dunahees should move on. It was a cruel assault on the Dunahee Search Centre.

"Michael's fate is not known," it stated. "After a year the odds are very much against him ever being found alive…the work of the search centre is done. It is time."

Many people were enraged by this insensitive piece of writing, but the most amazing part was what followed its publication. The response was overwhelming and nothing short of incredible. A barrage of readers' letters to the newspaper arrived, all commenting on the piece with headlines such as: The Search is Definitely Not Over; Column is Immoral; Response is Callous; Opinion Disgusting; Column a Sad Disgrace; A Poison Pen. The community was incensed, and considered the writer's remarks appalling, cruel and inappropriate.

People wrote:

"The search is definitely not over yet. We know how big the continent is and we have barely scratched the surface of some regions."

"Please do not speak of odds. Research existing abduction cases before you offer an opinion as to Michael's fate."

"How can you say there is no hope? Missing children have been located years later by organized groups. By ending the search or by closing the Search Centre will not ease Bruce and Crystal's pain.

Only Michael's return will do that. The pain of losing a child never goes away. I find your opinion unfeeling and callous."

"The Dunahee case has gripped the Greater Victoria community like nothing else could. The plight of the Dunahee family has moved us all. We are a closer, more caring society now because of this. Michael must be found."

"I have put in time at the Dunahee Search Centre. When a child is abducted, there is no little handbook that instantly appears full of direction and advice. No guidelines. The majority of people who are here have never volunteered before, so we're a little rough around the edges. Nobody gets paid to be here. But these people are 'real people' and they have a lot of heart. I am not quitting or giving up, and I thoroughly resent your uninformed, unresearched, and repulsive opinions under the auspice of journalism."

"We care and support the Dunahee family and will continue to do so as long as we are asked."

But objections to the column were not just from the local community. One letter also arrived from Denise Etchart Cooper, the executive director of the Kevin Collins Foundation for Missing Children in San Francisco. She wrote:

"Shame! Great shame on you! Michael Dunahee is a child, not some lost puppy whose disappearance must be reconciled and archived to make room for fonder memories. I am so outraged I can barely speak. But speak I must, and where to begin…believe it or not, the world does not begin and end in Esquimalt. Although it may have seemed so a year ago, Michael was not the first child to receive such extraordinary grassroots support…but the level of consciousness achieved in your area will sadly fade with time if left unprodded…And the implication that it can be "overdone" is outrageous. How can maintaining a raised consciousness about kidnapping hurt a community?

There are many cases of children being returned alive from long-term abductions. We cannot fold up our search simply because the odds are against it. We must pull together to stack these odds."

The letter continued along similar lines, quoting statistics and passionately stating that Michael and all missing children everywhere will never be forgotten. No one should ever give up until an answer is found.

It seemed that a community, a country and an entire world were supporting the cause. No one believed it was time to give up then. No one wanted to lose hope. No one wanted to stop believing. And, in all the years since then, nothing has changed. Every year, as yet another anniversary comes around, that initial belief is still alive. No one has let go. It was not time then and it is not time now, and it never will be until an answer is found.

Around the time of that first anniversary of Michael's disappearance, John Walsh of *America's Most Wanted* sent a letter of encouragement to the family and all those working at the Dunahee Family Search Centre. Those words, written in 1992, are as meaningful today, over twenty years later, as they were back then.

He stated that after all the initial media hype is over, all that is left is simply the courage and perseverance of parents of missing children who are determined to keep the child's name alive and forever in the public eye. That alone is a mammoth task. Who could possibility deny them that?

John Walsh's letter was an inspiration to all those working at the original search centre, and his words continue to inspire those who still keep the hope alive today.

March 20, 1992

To Bruce and Crystal, Friends, Supporters and Volunteers at the Michael Dunahee Search Centre.

God bless you on your most difficult effort to keep the search for little Michael alive. After a few months when a child remains missing, all the media often seems to die down and the real pain and heartbreaking work of trying to find out what happened to your child sets in; and unfortunately it often boils down to the sheer courage and perseverance of the parents to keep the child's name alive. That is what you are doing, and wherever Michael is he knows that.

God bless you. Be strong and be kind and be gentle to each other.

Warmest personal regards.
(Signed)   John Walsh.

P.S. A special thanks to all the people who are helping the Dunahees in their desperate search.

And then, on Sunday, March 22, 1992, two days before the first anniversary of Michael's disappearance, a miraculous thing happened—instead of just 100 people, over 1,500 turned out to run or walk to support the Dunahee family. People came from everywhere and from all walks of life. They ran, they walked or they pushed wheelchairs and buggies through the streets. They brought seeing-eye dogs and toddlers in strollers—even a parrot was seen!

Joan Geber and her fourteen-month-old son ran with the aid of a specially made baby stroller for runners. She stated that she and her son had run in other races in the past but the Dunahee event was very special to her as a mother.

"It's very near and dear to my heart," she said. "This is a family thing and I really feel what the Dunahees must be going through, even though I've never met them."

Most members of Crystal's Hellcats team ran that day and one of her teammates, Corinne Timmermann, said that participating in the run was simply part of the support all the team members had offered to Crystal since Michael's disappearance.

Although billed as a "fun run," medals were still handed out for the first man and first woman to cross the finish line. Mike Fox from Victoria took the medal for the first man to cross the line with a time of about 15 minutes, and sixteen-year-old Shannon Bowles was the first woman to finish.

It was a very emotional and satisfying experience for organizer Scott Johnson. Scott almost broke down as he congratulated all the participants at the end of the day.

"It's what I have always known about Victoria," he said. "This sends out a strong message to those who would come to this city to take our children. Our children are not toys...they will be treated with nothing less than the respect and dignity they deserve, and Victorians will see to that. What happened to Michael Dunahee must never happen again."

It was predicted then that the run would become an annual event; which proved to be true. Sure enough, the following year, in March 1993, almost 2,000 people registered for the run, which had been moved to the Esquimalt Recreation Centre. In the months following the first run Scott was hired by the Township of Langley on the mainland to work in their Recreation, Culture and Parks Division, and with his move over there he was no longer able to be "hands-on" leading up to the event. However, it had always been his intention to hand over the organization of the run to the Dunahees once he had it up and running that first year. Appreciative of Scott's initial groundwork on the project, Crystal and Bruce were pleased to carry on with the fundraiser. It was a natural evolution for the run to be moved to the township of Esquimalt, the community from where they all originated. Even though he had moved away, Scott remained involved and, as the founder, he was invited to every run to speak about the purpose of the event and to wish all the runners good luck.

The Esquimalt Recreation Centre hosted the Saturday evening dance for about three years, after which it was moved into the new Archie Browning Arena on Esquimalt Road because the dance floor was larger and allowed for many more people to attend.

Two years later, on Sunday, March 20, 1994, all the proceeds from the run and the dance that year—$10,000—went to Child Find. With Child Find having been so strongly involved in the search for Michael since the beginning, it seemed appropriate to transfer the money raised to that organization.

Bruce was greatly heartened by the response in 1994, particularly from Esquimalt residents where both he and Crystal had grown up. Among the runners that year was Labour Minister and Esquimalt-Metchosin MLA Moe Sihota. It was good to know that their own community was behind them in their determination to find Michael.

"These people will help us make sure that this kind of thing doesn't happen again," said Bruce.

Bruce by then was working full time at the Michael Dunahee Command Centre, which had been moved from the Legion basement, first to a room at the Tourist Bureau in the Esquimalt Plaza and then to the basement of his own home. He refused to give up.

"I'll keep on for as long as it takes," he said that year. "They would have found something by now. They would have found my son's body if he was dead. I believe that in two years if there was a body they would have found it…I know my son is still alive."

Scott voices his respect and admiration for Bruce and Crystal and their incredible determination.

"What stands out so strongly was the strength and courage of Bruce and Crystal. Talking about it naturally makes Crystal cry, but she was and still is a rock. She just needed to talk about it—to get it out of her system—almost every day, to the media and everyone else. She did whatever it took to get the word out about Michael. I will always be in awe of her courage and commitment to keeping Michael's story out there. That was why I chose that particular name for the run—Keep The Hope Alive. That's exactly what she did and still does to this day. I still believe Michael is alive and I believe in Crystal."

On one occasion, Scott and Bruce were sitting together in the local pub having a beer together prior to the run. They were discussing all the things that needed to be done when Bruce, who rarely showed the pain he was feeling inside over the loss of his son, began to talk about some tough, emotional topics. It hit Scott hard. Bruce had always been the tough one, what Scott described as "a soldier," holding back his emotions.

"As he talked, I was the one who started crying," said Scott. "Just couldn't hold it back. Bruce looked at me and basically told me to 'suck it up' and be strong. I knew he was right and that we had to get through this for Michael's sake, so I decided then and there that that would be the last time I would ever cry in front of my friend. I keep those tears to myself now; but year after year at some point after the event, usually when I'm alone, I just let it all out. It's sad, but so heart-warming that even after all these years, people still care and still believe. That's pretty special."

Following the great success of the 1994 Run, Crystal put out an early call to all elementary school-age children to help design a t-shirt to mark the fourth run, which was to take place on March 26, 1995. She wanted school children to be involved in the t-shirt design because to her it seemed appropriate to add a child's touch.

Children were asked to draw their own interpretation of a picture describing Michael being missing, but each design had to still contain an image of her son's face in the centre with the child's own design surrounding him. The design also had to include the full name of the event (the Michael Dunahee Keep The Hope Alive Drive 1995, 5-k Family Fun Run/Walk.) The entry deadline was January 15, 1995, and a prize was awarded to the winner, with the first name of the child whose design was chosen placed on the t-shirt.

At least sixty children entered the competition from a variety of local schools, including Macaulay Elementary in Esquimalt, Lake Hill Elementary School in Saanich, and Brentwood Bay Elementary on the peninsula.

Three years later, for the seventh annual run in 1998, Caitlin Dunahee, who was by then seven years old, designed the t-shirt. It showed a picture of her and Michael playing together in a playground.

As time passed, it became more practical to hold the accompanying dance on the Friday night of the run weekend, with the run itself taking place on the Sunday morning; and although the Dunahees like to keep the date as near to the anniversary date of Michael's disappearance as possible, other events being held around that time have often required pushing the date ahead into April. Nonetheless, support has never wavered. Crystal always begins organizing the event in January. Rising costs have meant an increase in the entry fee for the run, which has now risen to twenty dollars for adults.

In the year 2001, ten years after Michael's disappearance, close to 500 people were still participating in the annual run.

"This is a family event to celebrate community in the midst of tragedy," Scott Johnson announced to the media that year. "The story within the story is that people keep coming back ten years later. This run stands for hope. Each one of you brings hope to the family to never give up. Hope is so important. It's what it's all about."

Looking around at the sea of volunteers, runners, cyclists and even small children on their scooters, it was hard for anyone not to have hope. Ten-year-old sister Caitlin was racing around on her own mountain bike with her friends, while Crystal was being greeted with hugs and best wishes from her friends, acquaintances and strangers.

"It really helps us to pound the pavement for a while," Crystal said. "Now we're over the hump of the tenth anniversary and we will re-focus again. It is so good to see everybody out today."

More speeches were made that day, one by Steve Orcherton, spokesperson for Child Find BC, and another by then-mayor of Esquimalt Ray Rice, reminding people of the pain Michael's disappearance had caused so many people, and that still continued. Heads were bowed and tears flowed. It was an emotional moment, but the strong and unfaltering community feeling was a great comfort to the Dunahees.

It remains incredible to think that even though yet another decade has passed since that ten-year anniversary, people still come out to the run every Spring to support the Dunahees. Invariably the same people come out year after year to support the family, but there are also some new faces in the crowd each year. There are usually 200 to 300 participants in the run and 700 to 800 who attend the dance—those who pound the pavement or dance the night away in order to never forget Michael and to continue to raise funds to bring him and other missing children home.

It is inspiring to know that the initial proposal by a good friend has grown beyond anyone's expectation, with many other friends and colleagues taking up the call in subsequent years. Scott Johnson's original idea has become an event of enormous importance to the entire community of Greater Victoria. The proceeds now all go towards Child Find BC.

The twenty-first dance and run were held on April 6 and 8 of 2012 respectively. The Dunahees vow that the run to keep that hope alive will continue every year until an answer is found to the mystery of Michael's disappearance in 1991.

Why, indeed, would they stop?

CHAPTER 5

Child Find

We all share a common vision, that through hope and faith we can build a better future for our children and a place where our kids are safe and communities care.

—Steve Orcherton, Executive Director of Child Find BC

Within a few weeks of Michael's disappearance, Crystal returned to work and became the sole breadwinner in the family. This enabled Bruce, with help from his family, to take care of Caitlin and continue to work full-time at the search centre, which by then was situated in their new townhouse basement. It had been their original intention to move into a new unit, but when it happened it was not the happy event they had anticipated as a family of four. However, they were still in the same building in the housing complex, so at least it would be familiar to Michael when he came home to them. With Bruce continuing the work at the search centre, Crystal was not only able to support the family but, over time, expand her work with Child Find in their newly established office in Victoria.

By 1994, Crystal's obsession with her own son's disappearance had gradually evolved into her playing a much more active role with Child Find. It eventually was to become her passion in life. If her own son could not be found, she could at least assist other families who suffered the same pain of having a missing child. Maybe she could even prevent a similar tragedy from happening to someone else. Bruce's mother, Barbara Dunahee, also became very involved in Child Find, working alongside her daughter-in-law.

Child Find was created initially as a network of charitable, non-profit organizations across Canada to deliver services to families whose children go missing. It had its beginnings in Alberta following the disappearance of a six-year-old Edmonton girl in 1983. That same year, Child Find also was set up in British Columbia. In 1988, a formalized national voice was established with the formation of Child Find Canada. Child Find BC also opened a chapter in Kelowna in 1988, and in 1991, largely as a result of the Michael Dunahee disappearance, a chapter opened in Victoria, sponsored by the Organized Labour Council. Subsequently, satellite offices were opened in Prince George, Nelson, the Fraser Valley and Courtenay in 1998.

Today, more than twenty years after Michael disappeared, Child Find BC maintains its head office in Victoria with Steve Orcherton as executive director, Crystal Dunahee as president, and a board of directors. They now support eighteen community satellite offices throughout the province, and they are always looking for possibilities to establish more offices.

Child Find educates and advocates for the safety of children; assists in the location and recovery of missing children and reunites them with their legal parent or guardian; supports the families of missing children during the search; conducts public awareness campaigns throughout the year; undertakes community education in order to prevent the abduction and exploitation of children; and provides referral services to the families of missing children.

Their services include the distribution of missing children posters and flyers; free fingerprinting clinics across the country including an *All About Me* ID booklet for each child; detailed lists of safety tips and precautions for children and parents on the Child Find website; and ongoing awareness campaigns to educate the public on the growing concerns of child abduction and abuse.

The distribution of posters and flyers each year is expensive but well worthwhile, based on Child Find's philosophy that "the more people who see a photograph of a missing child, the greater the chance of recognition, leading to a greater chance of recovery."

In 2009 alone, over 12,000 children in British Columbia were fingerprinted, and since its inception, it is estimated that over one million children have been fingerprinted across Canada. Since 2009, the number has increased to 15,000 annually in BC.

The most vital link between Child Find and parents are the Child Find case managers, who work in conjunction with police and other support agencies across Canada. (BC's case manager is a volunteer position.) Upon notification of a missing child, Child Find goes into action by searching the extensive records and police databases that are available to them. Child Find can also recommend professional counsellors to help parents.

Child Find's work largely depends upon the support of the media, the corporate community, Canada Customs, Immigration Canada, and the average citizen who is willing to report leads or lend volunteer help. Many companies across British Columbia publish photos of missing children regularly in their newsletters and each Child Find office distributes photos through postings with Canada Customs, Canada Post, at malls and online. The Child Find mandate includes working closely with community groups and community policing to protect children and educate the public. Most recently the Tsawwassen Police department in BC has come on board with Child Find programs.

The RCMP, the Canadian Association of Chiefs of Police, the National Missing Children's Services in Ottawa, and the National Center for Missing and Exploited Children in Arlington, Virginia in the United States now all recognize and endorse Child Find.

Child Find BC does not receive any form of government funding. Without volunteers and donations, the organization would not be able to continue the never-ending work of printing missing children flyers, running fingerprinting clinics and identity programs, and paying the costs incurred in the recovery of a missing child. The annual operating budget of approximately $100,000 is all raised through year-round fundraising campaigns and donations made by generous individuals, organizations and corporations. Tax receipts are issued for any donation over ten dollars.

All funds raised from the Dunahee Keep The Hope Alive Fun Run go to Child Find, as do proceeds from the annual slo-pitch baseball Tournament of Hope held in August every year. The tournament was first conceived by a group of people sitting around a kitchen table and brainstorming ways to create financial support for the Michael Dunahee Search Centre. The first informal event was held on Labour Day 1991. The Victoria Labour Council originally sponsored the event, and teams had to be sponsored by a union with each team captain being a union member.

The Victoria Labour Council continued to organize the tournament from 1992 to 2007. When they unfortunately had to bow out in 2008, Child Find BC assumed that role. The Dunahee family, however, kept the same criteria in place for the teams; in that way the labour connection and broad labour support, which always played a major role in this charity fundraiser, has been preserved. BC trade union locals now sponsor twenty-four teams in the tournament. The twentieth event took place on August 6 and 7, 2011 at the Topaz Ball Park at Finlayson and Blanshard Street in Victoria; the twenty-first tournament was on August 11 and 12, 2012.

In the beginning, the tournament raised about $5,000 each year. In 2010 they raised nearly $10,000, and in 2011 the figure was between $14,000 and $15,000. This proud twenty-plus-year legacy of support from the trade union movement has raised well in excess of $100,000 for Child Find BC.

To raise additional funds, Child Find BC also sells children's Christmas cards, green ribbon pins for Missing Children's Day (May 25), Spirit of Hope bracelets and sun catchers.

According to Steve Orcherton, Child Find BC's services have been able to improve greatly during recent years, thanks largely to sponsors such as Shaw Communications, Alaska Airlines, DFH Real Estate, Kiwanis International, the Fraternal Order of Eagles, and Community Savings (the unions' credit union) along with the continued assistance of the labour movement. In addition, until 2011, Canon Cameras sponsored Child Find BC, with the generous donation of supplies such as ink and paper and taking children's digital pictures at the clinics where ID kits and fingerprinting services for children are offered to parents. Child Find BC recently purchased twenty-five cameras and printers in order to maintain the ID program throughout BC.

Crystal Dunahee is now the president of both Child Find BC and Child Find Canada. For Crystal, this has been an ongoing challenging, but ultimately rewarding, journey. In doing something positive for Michael and for other missing children, and by helping other families through the turmoil she understands only too well, her own pain has been made more tolerable.

Anyone wishing to volunteer at Child Find fundraising events or assist in any other capacity can call 1-250-382-7311 or 1-888-689-3463.

CHAPTER 6

The Media Challenge

I always felt rather like a salesman selling tragedy.

—John Carlow, Dunahee Search Centre volunteer and media coordinator

At the very beginning, with almost daily local and regional media interest in the Michael Dunahee case, there was no need to work to attract more attention to his story. And, inevitably, the Dunahees soon received requests from TV networks farther afield who also wanted to profile the story.

It was also never necessary to attract media attention around the anniversary of Michael's disappearance; there was always renewed interest in the case, which, in turn, always brought in new leads. Generating genuine new leads was the main goal of having media exposure; the more fresh and positive leads the better. Following the five showings of Michael's disappearance on *America's Most Wanted,* in late March and early April of 1991, numerous tips and sightings flooded in. The hope was that other TV shows might also bring in new, positive leads to assist the police.

However, there is a fine line between good media coverage and what is not; and it soon became apparent that the media could be both a help and a hindrance in the search for Michael and the ongoing police investigation. Stories were sometimes reported wrongly or portrayed inaccurately, causing unnecessary rumours to spread or generating leads that pulled the investigation off track and slowed it down. And if the media leaked a story too soon, it could jeopardize a promising lead the police might be investigating.

Among the earliest and most dedicated volunteers at the Dunahee Search Centre was John Carlow, who worked tirelessly to obtain good, ongoing media coverage for the Dunahee case and to keep the story in the public eye. He, more than most, can attest to the "blessing/curse" aspects of dealing with the media.

"I had come in, like everyone else, as a [general] volunteer," said John. "I went on the search teams, made flyers and answered the phones…but then I started to get more proactive as time went on. No one really knew what to do or where to go to pick up the pace. As the search centre efforts had to be clawed back financially, we moved to a smaller space and then back to the Dunahee family home to continue the work, and for a time, I also had an office in my own home."

Carlow dedicated over ten years to the cause of missing children in general, and Michael Dunahee's case in particular, through his work with Child Find BC and Child Find Canada, and the Missing Children's Society of Canada (MCSC) Western Region.

MCSC was created in 1986 in Alberta, and follows techniques developed by Marilyn Greene, a missing persons' investigator in the United States. Beyond advertising and poster distribution, they employ many other investigative procedures, such as having licensed investigators on staff and, when required, bringing in outside resources like field teams, cadaver dogs, and access to more investigators and international law experts. MCSC, like Child Find, is nonprofit but has a small paid staff and many volunteers working for it.

Rhonda Morgan, the founder of MCSC, initially spent a lot of time on Michael's case, during which time John Carlow came to learn a great deal from her about the management of missing child cases. He expresses great admiration for her work technique. After the search efforts for Michael were scaled back somewhat, John was offered a full-time position with MCSC and opened his own small branch office in Victoria. He worked for MCSC as a case administrator in BC from January 1998 until September 2001 when unfortunately, due to funding cutbacks, the BC branch had to close down.

Following the initial field searches for Michael, the search team—while still manning the telephone lines, attending vigils and local events and also handling the press—moved on to producing even more posters and making lists of where they should be distributed. But after the first two years, the attention given to Michael's disappearance began to lessen. John Carlow and other volunteers felt the necessity to step things up again. A decision was made to try other avenues and head in a completely different direction to gain exposure for the Dunahee case. Having become overwhelmed by the size of the North American media market, they tried instead to target specific places where images of Michael and his story could be placed, with the intention of re-focusing the distribution of information further afield, in smaller, regional, community publications in BC, and new places such as campgrounds, laundromats and many out-of-the-way spots.

The main objective was always to get more exposure for the Dunahee case, but no one was an expert on the subject of missing children. There was no guide on how to deal with investigators, the scam artists, or the other searching families. There was no magic formula for what should be said in front of a camera or to a reporter or on a live TV show, which might bring in the necessary information needed, that one tip that would lead to discovering what had happened to Michael. In those days everyone learned by trial and error. Writing speeches, compiling press releases, and attending press conferences were things the volunteers had to learn. Many mistakes were made at first, but everyone simply focused on finding a resolution to Michael's case and maybe helping other families at the same time.

During this time, John frequently asked himself, "Who am I to be sitting in this living room where a family has had their child taken from them? What am I doing here? How can I, or anyone else, put myself in their place? Am I really helping?"

John began to do more research, trying to find information on how other non-profit agencies had dealt with such cases. Frequent consultation with other case workers and missing children societies throughout Canada and across the States, some of which were just being run out of people's homes, became vital. He discovered that most of them were formed initially because of a child's abduction in their own area. Getting to know members of the RCMP Missing Children's Registry in Canada and those who worked at the National Center for Missing and Exploited Children in Virginia was also necessary. There was a need to constantly pick other people's brains and absorb all the knowledge that was possible. But it never seemed to be enough.

Ongoing communication with other non-profit agencies enabled the search centre to learn what shows were planning segments on missing children and to ask if they would consider including Michael's case. Unfortunately, some of the TV shows seemed more interested in just increasing their ratings, rather than giving consideration to a distraught family. At one particularly painful taping at the Dunahee family home, a crewmember took John aside and asked, "What would set the mother off...you know...particularly make her cry?"

John was appalled by this insensitivity; but he also knew it was their job to attract more viewers to their show and sensationalism did that. Ratings were everything. The Dunahee case had been described as having all the right ingredients or "saleable attributes" for a good show: a small, blue-eyed, blond boy; a grieving Canadian family (which appealed to US markets); and the fact that it was a true stranger abduction.

"I always felt rather like a salesman selling tragedy," John Carlow admitted. It was not a good feeling.

And the media could be cynical, many times making it clear they believed it more than likely that Michael was dead. Dedicated volunteers asked themselves how people could be so insensitive to other people's grief. Hope was the only thing keeping the Dunahees going, so why would anyone deny them that? Hope was also what kept volunteers such as John steadfast to the cause.

For the Dunahees, TV was always the most difficult. Television interviews were notorious for probing, and this meant the Dunahees were under a microscope and more brutally exposed to the whole world. Sometimes they would have to appear in the company of other families with missing children whose stories were equally tragic. There was always more emotion, more tears, and every time each family was analyzed and dissected. What was the family's background? Were secrets being withheld? Would something be discovered that they didn't want known? Why were they so quiet? Why didn't they cry? Why were they crying so much? Was it genuine or false? It became nothing more than a cruel intrusion into their lives. They became the victims who were being victimized because they were so vulnerable.

Nevertheless, Crystal appeared on many shows. *The Dini Petty Show* and *Missing Treasures* with Al Waxman in March 1992, and *Missing Children* with Sandie Rinaldo in 1995 seemed to emerge from media resurgence on the missing child issue. With a renewed interest in the subject in general, many older cases of missing children also received some benefit from all the publicity Michael's disappearance brought about. There were very few stranger abduction cases at that time, so Michael's case was rare. However, on the opposite side of the coin, some families of missing children expressed concern that Michael's case always obtained the lion's share of publicity, whereas their own particular child's case was passed over.

Prior to Crystal appearing on the *Oprah* show in the early nineties, a press release was sent out to the media, but the day the show was due to be broadcast, the missing children segment was pulled and rescheduled. The search team was not informed of this change in advance, only later learning that it was because a child's body had been found in one of the other missing children cases being profiled on the show. That change caused something of a nightmare for the Dunahee team, however, who were blamed for not communicating with the local newspapers more speedily.

An appearance Crystal made on the *Geraldo* show in January 1993 in New York, came about through an earlier meeting with Harry Monue, then a Victoria reporter with CHEK TV. It was an emotional show about missing children. Crystal was told that she was actually the first, and only, person to make Geraldo cry on air. On that occasion, Crystal also met John Walsh of *America's Most Wanted.*

One of Crystal's TV appearances was on KOMO television in Seattle on the *Northwest Afternoon Show* in January 1994. She appeared on the show with psychic Sylvia Brown, and Brown made many predictions concerning Michael's disappearance, saying she could see him surrounded by water and trees. As he had been born and lived in British Columbia on an island for the first four-and-half years of his life, this was not too difficult to imagine. But she also said that she could currently see him in Torrance, California, and she felt sure he would be home again with his family within the next twelve to eighteen months.

"I'm taking it all with a grain of salt," Crystal said at the time. "We can't say if this prediction is true or not."

Bruce was also somewhat cynical about this prediction, as he had been chasing down many other psychic leads from the very beginning. With police co-operation, he travelled to New York and Wyoming respectively during 1991 and 1992, following what seemed at the time to be promising psychic visions—but all to no avail. Having experienced some disreputable psychics howling at the moon or using other suspicious means to connect with Michael's abductors in their attempts to find answers, he had earned the right to be dubious about Sylvia Brown's latest prediction.

However, Sylvia Brown was very well known and respected in the US and many people had contacted the Dunahees through those first months to say they should talk to her. It was Bruce's mother, Barbara, who finally decided to write to the producers at the Seattle television station KOMO and arrangements were made for Brown to make her prediction on air in front of Crystal.

Crystal admitted that Sylvia Brown sounded genuine and "didn't come across as a wacko." In fact, Crystal's birth mother, who lived in Anaheim, California, arranged to send maps of Torrance to Victoria so that Crystal and Bruce could follow up this possibility. Sadly, this was just one more investigation that came to nothing.

There were other requests from shows such as *Hard Copy* and *Canada AM,* some of which never aired and some, even after seven hours of taping, only used an eight-minute segment on air. Nonetheless the word was spreading and that was the main purpose.

Certainly all this stubborn persistence might well have helped in getting the Dunahee case shown on the bigger shows like *Geraldo* in New York City and *Oprah* in Chicago. (Both shows paid all expenses for one or both parents to travel to them.) Maybe it was false hope that one of these shows might generate just one tip that might be the needed piece of information to find Michael, but it was always worth a try.

Some newspaper and magazine reports spoiled a new lead by splashing it across a front page—they all wanted to be the one that would help "tip the hat" to a recovery. It was frustrating for the police when what could have been a hot lead was leaked in the press and sensationalized.

Maclean's magazine, however, did a very thorough story on the Dunahee case, doing their own research and making Michael's story a part of a larger issue on missing children in general. The Dunahee story also appeared in *Homemakers* magazine and *People.*

A local Victoria magazine, *Focus on Women,* also ran an excellent piece on Crystal, and that three-page spread proved just as valuable as a *Woman's Day* issue that devoted a one-inch margin piece in a mass media print market.

At one point, frustrated because of the lack of results in spite of all the effort being expended, John Carlow decided to take a self-financed trip to California to talk with people at three well-established non-profit agencies, two in San Jose and one in San Francisco.

The people in San Jose were very helpful. They were more experienced in using posters and the media and they also had some very good connections with people who were knowledgeable in locating missing children. One agency in San Francisco had been described as the only organization that focused mainly on stranger abductions, so John hoped he would learn a lot from them; but, sadly, there was little they could offer that he did not already know. He also spent time at the Kevin Collins Foundation for Missing Children in the Tenderloin district of San Francisco and received support and advice from them. While John ultimately felt vindicated in going on his trip, it still did not supply the "vital key" needed to unlock the mystery of how to generate good, effective publicity that would help to find Michael.

Back in Victoria, one day in early 1994 John received a call from actress Winona Ryder, who at the time was coming to Victoria to make the film *Little Women,* which was to be filmed between April and June. Earlier, John had left his phone number with Winona Ryder's agent to contact him because of her advocacy for missing children. He hoped she might be willing to meet with the Dunahees, and he bluntly told her that he wanted to "use her fame" to help regenerate attention to Michael's case. While Ryder initially seemed receptive to the idea, ultimately it never panned out. He thought the reason might have been because her connection to the Polly Klaas abduction case in October 1993 had made it too hard for her to become close to another missing child story.

Twelve-year-old Polly Klaas was taken at knifepoint from an overnight slumber party with friends at her mother's home in Petaluma, California. Over the next two months 4,000 people helped search for her, and TV shows such as *20/20* and *America's Most Wanted* also covered the kidnapping. Winona Ryder, who also hailed from Petaluma, offered a $200,000 reward for Polly's safe return.

A palm print from sex offender Richard Allen Davis had been found in Polly's bedroom. Davis had a long criminal record and at the time was a wanted man with an "all-points bulletin" (APB) on him for a violation of his parole for a previous crime.

Police officers had, in fact, already encountered Davis in a nearby rural area when his car became stuck in the mud. Unaware of the APB, the local police released him after calling in his driver's license number to a dispatcher and learning it only showed his driving record and not any criminal record. Soon after this, it is believed he drove to the isolated spot where he had been holding Polly captive for weeks and killed her by strangling her with a knotted cloth. He buried her in a shallow grave.

On November 30, during a routine patrol check, the police finally arrested Davis for violation of parole and, quite by chance, the arresting officer happened to recognize him from police sketches of the suspect in the Polly Klaas abduction. He was immediately charged with kidnapping. Four days later, he agreed to lead police to Polly's grave near an abandoned sawmill in Cloverdale, California. He claimed he had been about to free Polly, but after the police had talked to him when his car was stuck in the mud he figured they were on to him, so he said he had to kill her.

On August 5, 1996, Richard Allen Davis was convicted of Polly's murder and sentenced to death. At the sentencing, Judge Thomas C. Hastings proceeded with the formality of the death sentence and then added, "Mr. Davis, this is always a traumatic and emotional decision for a judge. You, however, made it very easy today by your conduct."

The reason for the judge's statement was simple. When the jury had delivered their guilty verdict and recommended the death sentence, Davis stood up and gave the finger to the whole courtroom. Later, at his formal sentencing, he made malicious statements about Polly's father, implying that he had been molesting his daughter for years. Polly's father was distraught and he left the courtroom in disgust. Davis is still on death row in San Quentin State Prison, California.

During the two months between Polly's abduction and her murder, John Carlow had spent a few moments with Polly's mother in California while in the area working with another non-profit society on Michael's case. Another case worker had introduced them. Mrs. Klaas asked John about Michael and what was happening on the case. After he told her the details she said, "If they have been looking that long and still not found him...we will never find Polly."

Polly's father, Marc Klaas, became an advocate for missing and murdered children and established the KlaasKids Foundation. He made himself available to parents of kidnapped children and appeared frequently on *Larry King Live, CNN Headline News,* and the *Nancy Grace show.* Five years after Polly's murder, a performing arts center in Petaluma was named in her honour.

Against some opposition from her production people, Winona Ryder also insisted on dedicating the movie *Little Women* to Polly because she knew it had been the little girl's favourite book.

As a result of Davis's lengthy criminal record, ending in the kidnapping and murder of Polly Klaas, public support was galvanized for the 1994 "three strikes" initiative in California. This law requires the court to impose a life sentence on people convicted of three or more serious or violent crimes.

The Winona Ryder story became just one more episode in a long line of attempts to obtain publicity for Michael Dunahee's case. Certainly everything possible had been tried.

Even private investigators had approached the case from time to time, but they used "tracking by material trail" methods and in Michael's case there was, of course, no trail to follow. No evidence, no witnesses, no crime scene all added up to no trail to track.

People also frequently approached Crystal and Bruce with various devices such as safety guides and other crime prevention items, all looking for endorsements of their product. There was always someone out there hoping to benefit financially from Michael's abduction. Again, it was a case of the victims being victimized.

Despite all the publicity across North America and around the world, over ten years went by with no result. It seemed unbelievable that a child could have been snatched from his parents in plain sight, without anyone seeing it happen or knowing what had become of him.

Back in 1991 there was no one in Victoria or indeed across Canada who had not heard the name "Michael Dunahee." The publicity covering the case had been nothing short of gargantuan. In November 1991, the National Centre for Missing and Exploited Children (NCMEC) announced that 55 million flyers concerning Michael had been distributed throughout the world. How could anyone not know his face or know what had happened to him? It seemed impossible.

In 2001 Michael would have been fourteen, just a few years short of adulthood. By then, he might be dealing with memories of his first four years. He might have been questioning his roots. Sooner or later he would need to get answers from the people who had raised him since he was taken. He might need some kind of identification or some paperwork for medical purposes; and if it was missing or did not seem to add up, perhaps a red light would go on with the authorities.

That same year when her son would have been approaching manhood, Crystal made another TV appearance, this time on the *Vicki Gabereau* show in Vancouver. The media was still the best way to keep Michael's story alive in the hearts and minds of the masses.

Amazingly, Bruce and Crystal were still optimistic, holding out hope that Michael was out there somewhere. News had just reached them that year that a twenty-two-year-old young man, abducted as an infant from a New York hospital, had been found and returned to his parents.

"You see, it could happen," Crystal said in a *Victoria Times Colonist* interview. "No matter how much time goes by, there can still be a happy ending."

Losing a child is every parent's worst nightmare, but to still not know what happened to him ten years later is inconceivable. The Dunahees still believed their son was alive. They refused to consider anything else.

Spreading the word via the media for over ten years had certainly helped; and even though it had not provided the answer to Michael's disappearance, nonetheless, no one had given up hope. John Carlow, who had been among the many who helped instigate much of that early media attention, remains convinced that one day the truth will be known.

Naturally there are always doubters. To them, however, Carlow still gives the same reply today when he is asked what he thinks might have happened to Michael. It is a simple and clear conviction: "Show me evidence for any scenario that cannot be argued and I will agree to your conclusions. However, with no evidence at all, we have to believe that Michael is still out there somewhere, much older of course, but with a family still searching for him. It's happened before [a miracle] so we have to allow this family the same hope."

Victoria's Inner Harbour. Image I-03086 courtesy of Royal BC Museum, BC Archives.

Crystal and Bruce holding their newborn, Michael, May 12, 1986.

Bruce and Crystal pledge their love,
October 8, 1983.

Michael's christening, June 1986.

Michael as a toddler under the watchful eye of "Blue."

Michael's Auntie Karen holding her "little angel."

"Daddy's special boy," age 2.

Michael and Grandma H (Crystal's mom, Helen Caldewell).

iking with Mom.

Grandpa Dunahee showing Michael, age 2, how to use his gift from Santa.

Michael holding Caitlin at her christening in 1991.

Michael thought Caitlin would enjoy watching cartoons on TV with him. (Caitlin's favourite photo.)

Grandma Dunahee teaching Michael, age 4, all about safety on the water.

Michael, age 4, loved to picnic with
Grandma and Grandpa Dunahee.

oing fishing with Grandpa Dunahee and learning how to pilot the boat.

Everything tastes better at the beach! (Michael age 4)

Michael, age 4, with the catch of the day.

Blanshard Elementary School Playground, the area where Michael vanished on March 24, 1991.

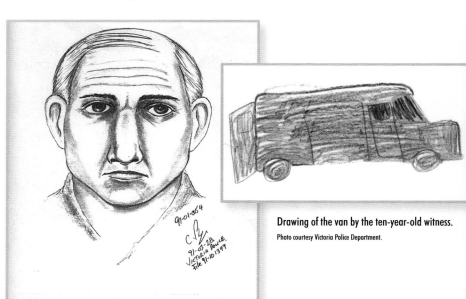

Drawing of the van by the ten-year-old witness.

Photo courtesy Victoria Police Department.

White Male, Late 30's to early 40's, 5'4" - 5'7", med. to chubby build, 150-160 lbs., shortish whitish grey hair which is very thin on top (almost bald)-receding and combed to one side, big nose and big ears, wearing a blue jacket with a white stripe across the front and grey rugby pants.

Composite sketch of the first person of interest identified in the case.

Photo courtesy Victoria Police Department.

MISSING

MICHAEL DUNAHEE

Last seen March 24th, 1991 at
Blanshard School Playground, Victoria, British Columbia

Michael has blonde hair, blue eyes, is 4½ years old, 3 feet tall, and weighs 35 pounds. He was last seen wearing a blue hooded jacket with red lining and red cuffs, T-shirt with four Mutant Ninja Turtles on the front, multi-coloured rugby pants, blue runners and Mutant Ninja Turtle underpants.

ANYONE WITH INFORMATION PLEASE CONTACT:
**Victoria Police Department — (604) 384-4111 or
Crimestoppers — (604) 386-8477**

A beloved photograph of a happy time becomes the missing child poster.

First Keep The Hope Alive Run, 1992, at Cedar Hill Recreation Centre with emcee Linden Soles welcoming crowds. Photo courtesy Scott Johnson.

Mayor Murray Coell of Saanich presenting prizes to the winners. Photo courtesy Scott Johnson.

The poster for the first run, the year following Michael's abduction. Photo courtesy Scott Johnson.

Saanich Parks and Recreation

MICHAEL DUNAHEE

KEEP THE HOPE ALIVE DRIVE

5K FAMILY FUN RUN

SUNDAY, MARCH 22, 1992   VICTORIA, B.C.

Location:	Cedar Hill Recreation Centre
Date:	Sunday, March 22nd, 1992
Distance:	5K
Start Time:	11:00 a.m.

Cost: •

Family Rate (5 members of immediate family):
Must have same last name. Includes T-Shirts: $40
Adults: with T-Shirt $10/ without T-Shirt $ 8
Child: with T-Shirt $ 8/ without T-Shirt $ 6

• Before March 10th

RUN FOR

THE MICHAEL DUNAHEE SEARCH CENTRE

INFORMATION: Scott Johnson, B.A. Race Director: 478-8782 (home); 595-7121 (work)

Crystal, Caitlin and Mavis Jenks (Crystal's birth mother) displaying the t-shirts for the third run in 1994.

Photo courtesy Victoria *Times-Colonist*, photographer Debra Bash.

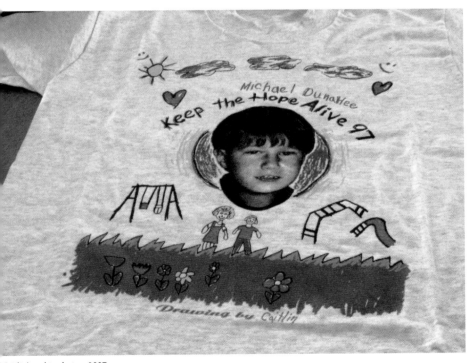

Caitlin's t-shirt design, 1997.

Insets: Age-progressed photos of Michael;
top: age 8; middle: age 17; bottom: age 26.

Photos courtesy National Centre for Missing & Exploited Children.

Tree of Hope still thriving in 2011. Author's collection

family still together, still strong: Bruce, Caitlin, Crystal
nd Caitlin's dog, Nyla; autumn 2008.

Crystal and Caitlin, best friends, autumn 2008.

Crystal and Bruce renewed their vows on their 25th wedding anniversary in October 2008.

A proud moment: Caitlin's high school graduation, 2008.

Caitlin's tattoo for Michael.

76

...ystal's meeting with Prime Minister Stephen Harper, May 2011. PMO photo by Jason Ransom.

...rystal receiving Order of BC October 4, 2011.
...oto courtesy Steve Orcherton.

The green ribbon of hope for the safe return of missing children everywhere.

L to R, Bruce, Crystal and Steve Orchertor executive director of Child Find BC, at 20? Tournament of Hope.

Crystal putting the finishing touches on a Child Find BC "All About Me" ID booth.

Crystal and Caitlin Dunahee and Steve Orcherton at a Child Find ID Clinic booth.

All photos this page courtesy Child Find.

Bruce Dunahee thanking everyone for participating in the 2012 *Keep The Hope Alive Run*.

Esquimalt Mayor Barb Desjardins, greeting the crowd at the 2012 run.

Steve Orcherton addressing the gathering at the 2012 run on behalf of Child Find BC.

Registration for the 2012 run. Even after twenty-one years, it is still busy.

Crowd gathering for the beginning
of the 2012 run

L to R, Caitlin, her cousin Samantha and
her Aunt Dorothy before the 2012 run.

Author with Crystal and Bruce Dunahee at 2012 run.

CHAPTER 7

No Reprieve

The sad thing is that I don't even know what his likes and dislikes are any more.

—Crystal Dunahee

Despite the ongoing worldwide exposure of Canada's largest-ever missing child investigation, the numerous fundraisers—including the annual Keep The Hope Alive Run and the Tournament of Hope baseball tournament in Victoria—plus a multitude of TV appearances by the Dunahees, fifteen years went by and Michael's disappearance remained a complete mystery. There were still no answers to the puzzle of a child who had simply vanished. The Michael Dunahee case by then was considered a "cold case."

By 2006, Crystal, when asked the same questions over and over again, sounded weary.

"Of course I still have hope," she always replied; but eventually she added, "but I have learned I can't live like that anymore. I don't want to get up on that emotional plateau each time a new tip comes in, where you're filled with hope and then you come crashing down again. I can't let myself go there anymore."

Then, in the summer of 2006, new life was injected into the case when the Victoria police announced that they had ten new solid leads into Michael's disappearance and would likely be sending two detectives to an unnamed BC town to interview a couple. This, of course, prompted a plethora of media reports and more telephone calls to the Dunahee home.

"That's what tends to happen every time the police talk about fresh leads," Crystal told one telephone interviewer. "We get phone calls from the media and it's really hard, especially when we don't know anything. That's why I don't even bother trying to find out what kind of tip it is. I just figure that if something big happens, the police will let us know."

In the early years, Crystal often spoke about the day her son would come home and how wonderful it would be. For many years, she kept his bedroom the same as it was on the day he vanished; it became almost a shrine to her missing boy. Even after the family moved, she still kept a room for Michael; but his toys and unopened birthday and Christmas presents were eventually put away in a closet.

"The sad thing is that I don't even know what his likes and dislikes are any more," she said. He would have turned twenty years old in 2006. Her little boy would have been a man by then.

While the Dunahees held steadfast to their hope, in the intervening years they also realized they had to try to get on with their lives. It was a difficult combination. When Caitlin was seven, they moved back to Esquimalt into a small wartime house, which they then demolished and completely re-built, and bought a franchise business— The Donair Shop on Esquimalt Road—at which they both worked, in addition to their day jobs. Working as many hours as humanly possible didn't give them much time to think—and that was the goal.

The year after Michael's abduction, Crystal decided to try and find her birth mother. She had known since she was ten years old that she was adopted, but it wasn't until 1992 that she decided to locate her birth mother by contacting the Reunion Registry in Vancouver, an organization that helps adoptees trace their roots.

"In the back of my mind, I had always wondered about my mother," said Crystal, "who she was, and did she miss me." The unbearable ache of losing Michael brought these feelings to the forefront again. She even wondered if, with all the publicity about Michael and her own constant appearance in newspapers or on TV, her birth mother might have seen her picture and recognized something in her face or felt a connection to her.

As it turned out, Crystal later discovered that her birth mother's brother-in-law, who happened to live in Duncan on Vancouver Island, had indeed noticed a resemblance between his sister-in-law and the mother of missing Michael Dunahee. Both Crystal and her birth mother share the same reddish-brown hair colour and blue eyes.

Eventually, the registry was able to find Crystal's mother, a woman named Mavis Jenks, who at that time was a fifty-one-year-old executive manager of a Tupperware business and living in Anaheim, California. Mavis had always hoped that one day the baby she had been forced to give up when she was only a teenager would find her. She had decided long ago not to try and track down her child for fear she would be interfering in another family's happiness.

It wasn't until Crystal reconnected with her birth mother that Mavis realized the relationship to the missing little boy from Victoria. In fact, the very next day after Crystal first contacted her by telephone, Mavis walked into a nearby store and saw a missing-children poster with Michael's among the many faces. It was an emotional moment, realizing he was the grandson she never even knew she had.

Crystal made plans to travel to California with Caitlin to visit her mother, and on July 14, 1993, they had an emotional reunion at Los Angeles International Airport. Meeting, for the first time, the daughter she had been forced to give up and her granddaughter was very joyful for Mavis, but the joy was tinged with sorrow knowing that she also had a grandson who had been missing for two years.

Mavis Jenks had given birth to Crystal at the old Victoria General Hospital in Fairfield in Victoria in 1961, not far from where Crystal had grown up with her adoptive Jeffries family. At eighteen years old, Mavis was a pregnant young woman with nowhere to turn for help. She well remembered the day she had given birth but, as was customary in those days when babies were being put up for adoption, the newborn was taken from the mother immediately. In Mavis's case, this happened even before she knew whether she had given birth to a boy or a girl. She only found out the sex of her baby because she happened to see that a nurse had written "girl, six pounds" on the chalk board in the delivery room, but by then the baby had already been taken away. Through the years she had tried to block out the memory of that painful experience.

Mavis left Victoria soon after the birth, only returning for brief visits to see a childhood friend. When Crystal finally found her in

1993, Mavis had been married for twenty-six years and had three other children by that marriage.

The reunion between Crystal and her birth mother was a happy one and finally gave Crystal something positive in her life. The two women discovered they had much in common, including the fact that they both enjoyed and had a natural talent for sewing. Crystal now had two families that supported her. Bruce often joked that he must be the only man in the world with three mothers-in-law: Crystal's birth mother, her adoptive mother, and her stepmother! (Her adoptive father had later remarried).

Another important development during those years was the production of a series of age-enhanced photos of Michael, first by the RCMP and then by the National Centre for Missing and Exploited Children in Virginia (NCMEC).

When a child is first reported missing, it is vital that the police have a complete description and a recent photo. Of course, over time the original photographs become outdated and obsolete, as a child is unlikely to be recognized if the image portrays a face that would by then be some years older. Age progression is used to create updated images for use on flyers and posters in order to verify sightings and to generate new leads for the police.

Age progressions have been used by NCMEC since the late 1980s as an effective tool to locate long-term missing children. The children are age progressed approximately every two years until they turn eighteen years old. From then, the child is age progressed every five years. According to NCMEC, the sole purpose of age progression is to "spark recognition" by the observer. The goal is to get the age-progressed image in front of people who interact with a missing child on a daily basis, as these people are the "new experts" on the child's face. To date, over 950 missing children who were age progressed have been safely returned to their parents.

The question often asked is how close the age-progressed image is to how the child would currently appear. To accomplish the goal of creating a face that someone somewhere will recognize, the child's genetic likeness must be preserved in the original age-progressed portrait and all subsequent age progressions. The NCMEC believes that roughly 80 percent of that genetic quality is in the eyes. The nose, mouth, facial shape and ears all work to tie the entire face together, but the eyes remain the most important feature. Hair and clothes are, of course, the least important.

"The human brain has a remarkable ability to 'fill in the blanks' regarding facial recognition," according to the NCMEC.

Computer photograph age progression is a fine combination of science and art, and enables a trained forensic artist with knowledge of facial growth characteristics to create a likeness of what the missing child might look like today. A forensic artist needs to see the best and most recent photograph of the missing child, plus photographs of the biological parents and siblings at or about the age of the missing child, and also, if possible, photos of other immediate family members. According to the RCMP and NCMEC, therefore, the ideal criteria for a computer photo-age progression are:

1. The child must be a minimum of two years of age.
2. The child must have been missing for a minimum of two years.
3. Photographs of the child taken as close to the day of disappearance as possible must be available, preferably a frontal view.
4. Photographs of the biological parents and/or brothers and sisters at the age the child's photo is being aged to should be provided.
5. Photographs of the biological parents and/or brothers and sisters at the same age as the child was when last seen, most suitably in the same position as the photo of the child, should also be provided.
6. Photographs may be in either colour or black & white.
7. Photographs should not be marked in any way. Comments should be attached on a separate piece of paper (for example, identifying the location of a specific scar).
8. The best photographs are the "school picture" type. The more photos available, the better chance the forensic artist has of obtaining a good likeness.

Sometimes the only available photograph from the family is of poor quality, but even then it is not entirely impossible for the artist to produce an age-progressed sketch. With today's technology, an excellent, high quality and even recognizable age-progressed face can be created from a photographic composite. The poor image can be used as a template from which the artist can blend generic facial parts from reference photographs, thereby creating an image of the missing child. A filter is placed over the final image to change it from a photographic quality to appear as a sketch. Many children have been recovered using this method.

Unfortunately, age progressing of missing infants cannot be done because an infant's face is too generic; recognizable characteristics are not apparent until at least two years of age. However, in a limited number of cases, the artist could possibly create a photographic composite of what the child *might* look like at a particular age if good quality photographs are available of both the infant's biological parents at or about the age the missing child would now be. But without having both parental photographs, no photographic composite would be attempted. Even between the ages of two and four years, often only a one-time age progression is attempted, as any additional attempts would amount to guesswork, which in turn could mislead authorities and the general public.

NCMEC artists are skilled in the area of creating recognizable faces as investigative aids to law enforcement agencies. These artists also provide training in this area to federal, state, local and foreign forensic artists at the University of South Florida in Tampa.

The first age-enhanced photo of Michael was reproduced in 1994, at which time he would have been eight years old.

In March 2006, the Victoria police announced a $100,000 reward in the Dunahee case and, at the same time, put out a new poster with another age-enhanced photograph of Michael as he might have looked at age eighteen. (By 2006 he would have been twenty.)

In the two months following the release of this new poster and photograph, over 500 more tips came in. Some were dismissed as being of no value, but most were thoroughly investigated.

In July, a tip came in from a Victoria couple that had recently travelled through Kentucky where they had seen a picture there of a young man who looked exactly like the age-enhanced photographs of Michael. Again, the lead was investigated but came to nothing. Fifteen years on, and still the same heartbreaking results.

By that time, Victoria police Detective Sergeant Al Cochrane was working the case, spending countless hours on a never-ending list of clues and tips.

"I still believe there is somebody out there who knows what happened to Michael and for whatever reason hasn't been able to come forward and say it," he stated in 2007.

Cochrane worked the case in addition to his full-time job in the financial crimes division. Although his job of solving cold cases was eliminated in October that year, he held on to the Michael Dunahee file, which by then represented an overflowing inbox of paperwork, plus other boxes and binders of material that cluttered an entire table in his office. Like a dog with a bone, he refused to give up.

"If I can, I try to come in at least one day a week to dedicate just to Michael's case. If it's at night, I try and stay late." He liked to pick a day when no one else was around, which helped with his concentration.

More than 450 of those initial 500 new tips following the release of the poster and the new $100,000 reward were soon cleared. Most of them were from people across North America who had seen someone who resembled the age-enhanced photo of Michael.

One lead concerned a man who was wanted on a Canada-wide warrant for two outstanding murders and who had escaped from an Alberta prison. He was said to have been living in Burnaby (near Vancouver on the mainland) around the time of Michael's disappearance. It was a hot tip but, again, it led nowhere.

Nonetheless during 2006 and 2007, police believed they were on the right track because they were working the case from a number of different angles, and officers even travelled across North America chasing down some of the leads.

Then, in January 2009, a Milwaukee TV station reported that police there had found an old missing-person poster of Michael inside the home of sixty-two-year-old Vernon Seitz, a known sex offender, who, just before dying, confessed that he had killed two children back in 1958. This was reported to the Victoria Police department and again was thoroughly investigated. However, any connection to Michael was dismissed as being highly unlikely.

"What's left is handling the annual flood of tips that usually come in around the anniversary date," stated Cochrane. "One day that one all-important eyewitness will decide to call the police.

"My first and foremost goal is to bring Michael home for his family and to bring some kind of peace to them." He added, "If something ever happened to one of my children, it would be important to me for closure."

Thus, fifteen years into the investigation, Cochrane and other dedicated investigators still worked to find the missing piece in a frustrating puzzle.

CHAPTER 8

The Twentieth Anniversary Year

It feels like we are stuck in a time capsule...

—Crystal Dunahee

2011 marked the twentieth anniversary of Michael's disappearance.

The annual Keep The Hope Alive Family Fun Run and Walk was held on April 10 in Esquimalt, with a dance at the Archie Browning Centre in Esquimalt preceding the run on April 8. All money raised from both these events went as usual to Child Find BC.

Songwriters Bonnie Chase and Laurie Fouracres wrote a special song for Michael to mark the twentieth anniversary. The Dunahees liked the lyrics and had them printed on all the t-shirts that year:

> Michael, hear your name,
> We'll find a way to end this game.
> Don't you ever feel alone,
> Don't give up; we'll get you home.
> We'll find a way to end this game.
> Michael, hear your name.

The Victoria Police Department also held a press conference in April 2011, which both Crystal and Bruce attended. Fighting back tears, Crystal Dunahee spoke from her heart, with Bruce at her side as always giving her the support she needed.

It feels like we are stuck in a time capsule, realizing that twenty years have gone by without the answers we want. We know someone is out there who knows what happened. We are asking them to come forward and pass on that information to help us find some closure.

A special occasion comes and goes and you always know that there's one person missing from the table. He's twenty-five now, so we've missed kindergarten and all the different steps through school to graduation...Is he married? Does he have children? It's the worst nightmare you can possibly imagine, one I wouldn't wish on anybody.

Alongside her were all the missing posters of her son: pictures of a small boy when he was a happy, blond child wearing a blue shirt and red bow tie. Crystal said he would have been due to enter kindergarten later in the year he went missing. If he was still alive somewhere, which they strongly believe is the case, what was he doing for a living? What had his life been like? Was he happy?

Deputy Police chief John Ducker, the only remaining Victoria police officer who originally worked on the case immediately after Michael's disappearance, also spoke at the press conference. He was a young constable at the time Michael went missing, and the case still haunts him.

"Someone out there is responsible," Ducker said. "That someone has lived with this burden for far too long and we encourage them to come forward today."

An article written by Tom Hawthorne for the *Globe & Mail* in March 2011 began with the words: "Michael Dunahee is the boy everyone knows but no one has met..." and went on to say that as of March 28, 2011, Michael had been missing for 7,311 days, more than half of which time Detective Sergeant Don Bland of the Victoria police also worked on the case.

Stated Bland, "If he is still with us, he doesn't know where he came from, or he thinks he was raised by people who are not really his true parents. If it has gone on this long, God knows how much longer it could go.

"Everything you can surmise might have happened is based on assumptions based on the balance of probabilities," Bland added. "After thousands of interviews and re-enactments, there's not a living soul who saw Michael disappear—except the person who took him."

By the time he retired in 2004, Bland had spent twenty-seven years in the police force, a career that began with walking a beat and ended with him being a detective with the major crimes unit, dealing with cases such as the abduction of Michael Dunahee. During those years he had seen it all, from arsons and domestic abuse cases to rapes and homicides. Nevertheless, he is by nature an optimist—a characteristic not many police officers can claim to possess because they deal mostly with the unpleasant side of life. His only wish before retirement had been to find a resolution to the Michael Dunahee case; however, that was not to be. The $100,000 reward has remained in place for anyone with information on the case.

"You can't close a file until you know you have the final answers. There is no ending yet," Crystal said at the press conference.

Bruce agreed, saying, "It's kind of nice to know that the police are as stubborn as we are. They don't want to give up and neither do we."

By 2011, Inspector Bob Gehl, head of the department's investigative section, was overseeing Michael's file. Victoria detectives had by then chased down thousands of tips. Two of the strongest were, in fact, more recent. In 2006 a tip had come in from Port McNeill, a small, thriving community with a population of 2,700 on the northeast side of Vancouver Island. Mountains, rainforest and the islands of the archipelago surround it. When word reached Victoria that a boy living in the town could possibly be Michael Dunahee, the media buzzed with the news. Police interviewed the young man and DNA testing was carried out, but once again the results proved he was not Michael.

Then, in early 2011, Chase, British Columbia became the centre of speculation. Chase, with a population of approximately 2,500, is a village located in the interior of British Columbia at the outlet of Little Shuswap Lake. When members of that community became convinced that a young boy who had moved there with his parents around the time of Michael's disappearance, bore a strong resemblance to him, the media was once more on the trail of this new lead. Again, the police investigated the report and DNA testing was undertaken; but in February 2011, they issued a press release stating that the boy was not Michael.

"I don't know how we get by," said Crystal when interviewed at the time. "It's just a matter of instinct. You don't give up. You continue going forward until you have that right answer."

Crystal simply relied on her own senses about her son.

"They do their DNAs," she said, "but I say, show me a picture and then I'll tell you. People were adamant in both the Chase and the Port McNeil cases, but I said, 'Don't waste your time.'"

On May 25, 2011, to commemorate International Missing Children's Day, and just thirteen days after what would have been Michael's twenty-fifth birthday, Crystal and Bruce travelled to Ottawa to meet with Prime Minister Stephen Harper and Justice Minister Rob Nicholson.

They were there to support a new online tool that they hoped would make it easier to find missing children and to prevent child abductions. The Canadian Centre for Child Protection had launched a website: www.missingkids.ca/ to raise awareness about International Missing Children Day, to highlight new missing-children cases, and also to draw attention once again to some of Canada's oldest and most painful cold cases. Families can register their missing child on the site and receive support from a trained caseworker using the latest technology to locate the child. Any tips that come into the website are automatically passed to the police for investigation.

People can also sign up to receive missing-children alerts if they want to assist in searching. The site also has a national missing-child database and information for both parents and children on how to prevent abductions.

"Each year, more than 50,000 children are reported missing in Canada," said Prime Minister Harper. "Our government is taking decisive action and working closely with groups, such as the Canadian Centre for Child Protection, to safeguard the most vulnerable and innocent members of our society—our children."

The prime minister talked with the Dunahees and with Diana Boland, whose three boys had been taken from her fifteen years earlier by their non-custodial father, and with Anthony Wood whose daughter, Sunshine, had been missing for seven years.

Boland's sons were taken by her ex-husband, Gary O'Brien, who simply called her to say that sons Adam, Trevor, and Mitchell (who were fourteen, eleven and four, respectively at the time) would not be coming home to her in St. John's. She asked to speak to them and was told by O'Brien, "Later." That one word had been giving her hope for fifteen years. She was still waiting, and she felt confident that the new missingkids.ca website would assist her and parents of other missing children.

Anthony Wood's daughter was last seen on February 20, 2004, in front of the St. Regis Hotel in Winnipeg. She was sixteen at that time. Wood had been looking for his daughter ever since, and he too hoped the new website would aid in that search.

Statistics show that there are fifty reports of "stranger abductions" in Canada every year, but the majority of missing children (75 percent) are still runaways, with girls more likely to run away than boys; but both genders tend to take off around the ages of fourteen and fifteen.

In Michael Dunahee's case, over twenty years is a long time to be searching for a little boy whose disappearance is a complete mystery, but Crystal firmly believes that the missing kids website has given new life to Michael's and other missing children's cases.

"We have renewed hope of receiving new information to help us find Michael," Crystal said in an interview at the time. Since they made their emotional appeal in April 2011, 100 more tips have been received, and they continue to come in.

In October 2011, the Dunahees launched the Michael Dunahee website: michaeldunahee.ca which also links to www.missingkids. ca/ as well as the Facebook community page *We Will Never Forget Michael Dunahee*. Michael's website includes all the pertinent material on the case, including videos, photos, maps, articles, plus a link to report a tip or sighting.

As well as launching the Michael Dunahee website in October 2011, Crystal and Bruce both celebrated their fiftieth birthdays with another fundraiser for Child Find BC, a dance at the Esquimalt Recreation Centre with approximately 100 people attending.

Today it is hard to believe that this middle-aged couple are the same people who had their lives so brutally exposed to the world twenty years earlier. In 1991, Crystal was a shy young woman just approaching her thirtieth birthday, wanting and expecting a normal life with her husband and two children. She did not seek the limelight. Today she is a poised, confident and somewhat pragmatic woman whose face shows the signs of a grieving mother. Bruce is no longer the fun-loving, dark-haired, debonair man he once was;

his hair is grey and he doesn't smile as much as he once did. Most days he wears a Keep The Hope Alive t-shirt, as though to keep his son close to his heart all the time. Mementos and photos of their son surround Bruce and Crystal throughout their home.

"Everything we do, we do for Michael," says Crystal.

October 2011 was also destined to be an important month for Crystal in yet another way. Child Find BC announced that, for her ability to "live through personal tragedy and become a community leader and advocate for services to families whose children go missing," Crystal Dunahee was awarded the Order of British Columbia, the highest honour that can be bestowed on a citizen of British Columbia. Lieutenant Governor Steven Point presented the award to Crystal at Government House in Victoria on October 4, 2011.

No one could have deserved this honour more.

CHAPTER 9

Sister in the Shadow

We are not just mother and daughter; we are best friends.

—Caitlin Dunahee

Michael's little sister Caitlin, whose entire life was drastically overshadowed by the events of 1991, turned twenty-one in September 2011.

She had spent the first six months of her life sharing a room with a brother of whom she has absolute no memory. But she knows his face well, as Crystal has always displayed pictures of Michael throughout the house with other family photos. She wanted Caitlin to know that he was still there with them, in spirit if not in person. Despite living in the shadow of overwhelming family tragedy, Caitlin has grown into a remarkably strong young woman who carries the memory of Michael in her heart.

She cannot remember when she first realized she had an older brother who had been abducted. She simply grew up with the knowledge and accepted it as a part of her life. She has been told that during the first months of her life, her big brother would love to watch her and could not wait for her to grow up so he could play with her. He would often gaze in wonder at her as she lay in her crib.

One Saturday morning when Crystal was busy elsewhere for a moment and Michael was watching cartoons on television, Caitlin, who was lying on the floor beside him on a blanket, began fretting, so Michael gently pulled her up onto his lap. When Crystal returned he told her that Caitlin had been crying because she wanted to watch the cartoons with him. He had held her in his arms very carefully so she could also see the cartoons. He knew he had to lift her with care. He was a wise little boy. And Caitlin had certainly stopped crying.

Today, Caitlin seems to know instinctively that Michael would have always been a kind "big brother" who would have constantly looked out for her needs. She feels cheated that she never had the opportunity to know him and to find out for sure what kind of sibling relationship they would have had.

Having the name "Dunahee" has often been difficult for Caitlin. Even more than twenty years later, the name is still well known and she often wishes it did not have the kind of recognition that is connected to it. She remembers one embarrassing incident at a grocery store when the checker noticed the Dunahee name on her credit card. The cashier asked if she was Michael Dunahee's sister and then proceeded to ask numerous questions, saying how sorry she was about it all. She probably meant well, but in the process of commiserating with Caitlin, she held up a line of shoppers and embarrassed a young girl. It was neither the time nor the place to discuss the fate of Caitlin's older brother or her theories as to what might have happened to him.

Caitlin knows and understands why her parents were overly protective of her as she grew up. As a toddler she was placed in reins to prevent her from running away. Unlike her big brother, Caitlin, being a more adventurous child, more than likely would have wandered off. Crystal often told her she was "the lion" in the family, where Michael had been "the lamb."

For many years, however, she could not fathom why her mother would constantly watch her. She remembers when she was about eight years old that Crystal would stand at the front door as Caitlin ran across the street to play at a friend's house that was in plain sight of their own. Her mother stood there until she was sure her daughter was safely inside the house—and then would still insist that Caitlin phone home when she got there.

Caitlin acknowledges, however, that her mother tried to give her as normal a life as possible. Crystal has always been very supportive and encouraged her daughter's potential in sports, such as skating, swimming, baseball and touch football. Caitlin has inherited both her mother and father's talents in many of those sports.

"My mom wanted to give me everything and beyond," Caitlin says. "She often over-compensated me I know."

Caitlin adds, "We are not just mother and daughter, we are best friends. I hate it when she cries, especially around the anniversary of Michael's disappearance. I find that hard to take.

"In 2009 we attended the wedding of Ben, the little friend Michael played with on that last morning. Mom found that very hard, as it was an emotional experience for her, perhaps imagining that this could have been Michael getting married that day. I know, however, that she was very happy to have been included in Ben's special day."

Caitlin's experience with her father has been somewhat different. While Crystal was drawing her daughter ever closer to her, Bruce seemed to be pushing her away. Bruce found handling his relationship with his daughter more difficult.

"Dad often tried to buy my love, but didn't seem to want any kind of real father-daughter relationship," Caitlin said. "It was strange and it wasn't until I was in middle school that he finally admitted to me one night that he had always been afraid to love me too much in case he lost me too. He was only able to say that after he had had a few drinks."

Caitlin seems to understand her father's pain, even though he broke her heart on many occasions because of his dismissal of her presence. Always trying to gain her father's approval, Caitlin tried hard to be the best possible student through school and to make him proud of her, but whatever she did it never seemed to be good enough. He expected his daughter to be a straight-A student or he wasn't satisfied. Even when she later scored an incredible 91 percent on a chemistry exam to enable her to enter an engineering program for university, Bruce's reply was, "What happened to the other 9 percent?"

For many years, Caitlin carried her own sense of guilt about Michael's disappearance that day. She wondered if her father resented the fact that he had been placing her in her stroller instead of going over to the playground with Michael—which is what he would have done had he not had to take care of Caitlin.

"I blamed myself for being there and for my dad having to watch me instead of being with Michael." It was a terrible and unnecessary burden for a child to carry.

Now that Caitlin has moved away and is living in Vancouver to pursue her post-secondary education, their father-daughter relationship has improved somewhat; but Caitlin regrets all the lost years and occasions when she and her dad could have been closer. In many ways the day Bruce lost Michael, he also lost his daughter.

During her teens, Caitlin, always a free-spirited child and much like her father, occasionally got into trouble. Through her middle school and high school years, she became rebellious and began running with the wrong crowd. Even when told certain things were wrong, she had to find out for herself. By age fourteen, she resented the fact that her curfew was much earlier than that of her friends. Many of her friends did not want to sleep over at her house because they knew the rules there were stricter. Eventually, however, Caitlin learned who her true friends were and appreciated them for understanding her family situation. She wonders if she might have avoided some of the trouble she got into if she'd had an older brother to talk to who could have given her advice and steered her away from some situations.

There have been other painful episodes for Caitlin. On one occasion at school another student said that the only reason she got good grades was because she was Michael Dunahee's sister and the teachers felt sorry for her. This really hurt Caitlin who worked exceptionally hard to obtain the good grades she received.

Later on, one of her boyfriends asked her, "When are your parents ever going to give up? They should have got over it by now and moved on with their lives." Needless to say, that boyfriend did not last long!

Like parents everywhere, Bruce and Crystal have not always approved of Caitlin's boyfriends, but they do like the young man she is currently seeing. His family lives close to the Dunahees in Esquimalt. He has moved to Vancouver to pursue post-secondary education and to be near Caitlin.

"Even my dad gets along with him," she laughs. "They trust him and enjoy his company."

After she left high school, Caitlin had planned to go to France for a year as a nanny, but when her plans fell through she worked in Victoria for a year while deciding what she wanted to do with her life. She worked at several jobs: skating instructor; summer camp leader at Esquimalt Recreation Centre; assistant at a seniors' home; hostess at Spinnakers restaurant; and as a clerk at a liquor store.

She decided to take courses in building technology at the Pacific Design Academy and acquired a diploma in house design. With that under her belt, she planned to become a civil engineer, but her year at Kwantlen Polytechnic University in Richmond (2011–12) convinced her that engineering was not for her. Preferring architecture, she was accepted into the architectural science program at BCIT where, with her already earned credits, she joined the second year of this program on a part-time basis in September 2012, attending full-time in January 2013.

Today Caitlin Dunahee seems driven to succeed, and there is no doubt that she will. Would she have been a different person had Michael not have been abducted? She believes she definitely would, but then again it is something she will never know, just as she cannot know whether her relationship with her father would have been better or the same.

Once the annual Keep The Hope Alive Fun Run began, it became a regular part of Caitlin's life. As she grew older, she was able to assist by handing out juice boxes to the runners, distributing flyers and helping with the registration. She and her Aunt Karen (Bruce's sister) still work together on many of these projects each year. Karen also helps at the dances by tending the bar, and now that Caitlin is old enough, she also attends the dances and tends bar.

Caitlin discovered a Facebook page had been set up entitled *Whatever Happened to Michael Dunahee?* Unfortunately, disrespectful people had begun to post cruel comments, so in May 2011 Caitlin created her own completely re-invented page.

Called *We Will Never Forget Michael Dunahee.* The page received approximately 7,000 hits in its first week. She regularly posts up-coming events that raise money for Child Find. Anything odd or malicious that is posted, Caitlin passes along to the detectives involved in Michael's case and they look into it.

Caitlin firmly believes that Michael is still out there somewhere, but she admits she has had many moments of doubt through the years.

"We just need answers," she says.

She does have some theories of her own though. For instance, she believes that if he was snatched by someone and then illegally sold for adoption, he might have been brought up in a family who could have brainwashed him into thinking he was their own. That family might today be living anywhere in the world and Michael would not readily remember anything that happened to him during the first four and a half years of his life.

"I try to think back to my own earliest memories," she says. "There is nothing that I can really recall with clarity before I was five. One memory I do have concerns waking up in the middle of the night and hearing my mom crying. I think it must have been around the anniversary of Michael's disappearance one year, and I was still quite small myself. I wanted to comfort her, so I got out of bed but knew I wasn't supposed to go downstairs in the middle of the night. Instead, I threw a roll of toilet paper over the railing for her to use as Kleenex.

"I also remember sitting by the window one day and learning to tie my shoes—and that must have been before I went to kindergarten, but it is not a really clear memory. Unfortunately, I don't recall the faces of people from my first few years, so would Michael? We would all be virtual strangers to him now, so how would he feel if he ever met us again?"

But, like her parents, Caitlin clings to the hope that Michael is still alive somewhere in the world and is happy and healthy.

It is the best she can wish for the big brother she never knew.

CHAPTER 10

Life Since 1991

No matter how much time goes by, there can still be a happy ending.

—Crystal Dunahee

There have been many changes in Michael's hometown of Victoria since 1991. The location from where Michael was taken looks a little different today. Although the building that once housed the Blanshard Elementary School on Kings Street is still there, it is no longer a school. In 2004 it was established as University Canada West (UCW), but closed down in 2011 and the building remains empty.

The portable classrooms once alongside the old school and the playground area are long gone, and the car park is much enlarged. The rocky outcropping next to the field, onto which Bruce climbed to look back and check on Michael, is also gone; it was blasted out many years ago. Different businesses occupy some of the buildings around the area and different people, for the most part, occupy the apartments.

The small "Tree of Hope," planted by the children of Blanshard Elementary School in 1992 on the first anniversary of Michael's disappearance, still stands there. Sadly, the plaque alongside it has become somewhat tarnished with age. Crystal says she intends to replace it one day.

Crystal and Bruce Dunahee have continued to organize the Keep

The Hope Alive Run around the anniversary of Michael's disappearance every year, and to support the Tournament of Hope in August; and they continue to be active in the missing children cause.

In 1993, after an absence of approximately two seasons, Crystal decided to return to playing women's touch football. Understandably, her team has never again played at the Blanshard School field. Crystal's friend, Donna, the Hellcats teammate she and Bruce picked up on the way to the game that morning in March 1991, passed away from cancer a few years ago.

Crystal no longer works in insurance, but is still involved in office administration work.

Bruce began taking jobs again two years after Michael's disappearance, when he was no longer working full-time at the search centre. In the winter of 1994, he accepted a three-month contract job installing carpets at the Blanshard Court apartments, just metres away from where his son had disappeared.

"That was the best way for him to confront what had happened," Crystal said. Prior to that, although they knew they would have to face it again one day, both Bruce and Crystal avoided the entire Hillside-Blanshard area. Even today they don't go by that area if they can avoid it; over twenty years later, the memories are still too raw.

Crystal also came to realize she could not walk around being despondent all the time because it would soon affect her daughter's emotional state.

"We tried to keep as happy an atmosphere as we could," she said. "As a little girl, she did know she had an older brother and every once in a while she'd pop out with, 'You've got two children, mummy, one is missing and one is me.'"

The hard work they put into their donair franchise has paid off, with one recent review of their shop making the claim, "It's the best donair in town."

In October 2008, on the occasion of Bruce and Crystal's twenty-fifth wedding anniversary, the couple renewed their vows to one another, disputing for all time the many rumours surrounding their marriage. It was surely the utmost allegiance they could have made to each other after having survived the greatest tragedy imaginable for any parents.

The Dunahee family has had a lot to work through to reach the point where they are today. Bruce had his own demons to fight because of the loss of his son—causing him perhaps to withdraw from both his wife and daughter—as did Crystal and Caitlin. They all dealt with Michael's loss in the way that was right for each of them. For Crystal, it was throwing herself into work with Child Find and assisting other families in their grief. For Caitlin, it has been working hard to gain her father's approval. For Bruce, it was working long hours to help ease his pain and bury his emotions.

There is no recipe for happiness in any family. It is just a question of dealing with things one day at a time as best as possible. The Dunahees had more to deal with than most, but despite all the odds against them, they have kept their family intact.

In 2002 Crystal lent her name in support of the AMBER Alert system to notify the police in cases of possible child abductions. In addition, Crystal still serves as president of both Child Find BC and Child Find Canada.

The effects of Michael's abduction rippled through the entire family. Bruce's sister, Karen Dunahee, had a close bond with Michael from the moment he was born. He was so happy-go-lucky and very laid-back. To her, he was a little angel, the true meaning of pure love. On the day Michael went missing she was at work, so she was unaware of what was happening until around five o'clock when her father phoned to let her know that Michael was missing and everyone was still at Blanshard Elementary School looking for him. Karen went straight there.

Like everyone else, Karen initially assumed Michael had wandered away and got lost. As the truth slowly sank in that he had been abducted, she felt numb. She could not comprehend how this could possibly be. Her little pal, the small boy she babysat and took out on little "dates" and whom she had loved like her own child, was gone.

Her sadness over his loss soon turned to anger and then depression. In 1993 she decided to move away from Victoria and try to make a new life elsewhere. She studied Early Childhood Education at North Island College, graduating in May 1994 and worked in daycare in the Courtenay area for five years. In 1999 she moved back to Victoria to be near her family again. After completing a contract with Club Med to work in their daycare program in the Dominican Republic, she returned to Victoria permanently in 2001. In 2009, she decided it was time for a career change and returned to school to study office administration. She and her partner now live in Esquimalt with her mother, Barbara, in Karen's parents' house.

Learning to accept and move on from losing Michael took a long time. Then one day while listening to the song *The Dance*[1] she realized that the joy of having such a special child in their lives for those brief years had been a gift; and it was only in learning to fully appreciate this gift that they had survived losing him. But why, she wondered, did they have to experience the loss at all? She has no answer to that question.

Karen never had children of her own, saying, "It was never the right time." She had dearly loved her nephew and is grateful she still has her two nieces, Caitlin and Hayley (brother Keith's daughter) in her life. The love of her nieces and her faithful dog, Blue, helped her through the worst times. Blue had loved Michael too, and always watched over him with special canine care when Michael was a baby.

Eerily, about a month before Michael disappeared, Karen, who is a very grounded and sensible woman, experienced a very frightening dream from which she awoke in a cold sweat. In the dream, she was out somewhere with Michael when suddenly he fell into a small hole, which then turned into a very deep well. Michael kept going down into the well, deeper and deeper, until she could no longer see or hear him. It was a horrible experience. Had it been a premonition? It is something she will never know.

She admits that the Dunahee family has never sat down together and discussed "theories" as to what might have happened to Michael on that fateful day. That would be too difficult.

Harvey Dunahee never recovered from the loss of his grandson. He had just begun to teach Michael to fish, and they both were looking forward to more fishing excursions. But after Michael's abduction Harvey never went fishing again; he never even looked at his fishing rods. Harvey took early retirement from his job as an engineer with the Canadian Coast Guard. He drank more than he probably should have. He was seventy-three years old when he died on March 28, 2011, four days after the twentieth anniversary of his grandson's disappearance, never knowing what had happened to Michael. Harvey was a life member of the Royal Canadian Legion,

---

[1] *The Dance* was written by Tony Arata and made famous by Garth Brooks.

Branch 172 in Esquimalt, where a Celebration of Life was held in his honour. In lieu of flowers, the family requested memorial donations be made to Child Find BC.

Michael's grandmother, Barbara Dunahee, dealt with Michael's loss by volunteering with Child Find. In the beginning she worked as an office organizer, sorting and stuffing envelopes, and mailing posters to various organizations. Eventually she became office manager. Barbara also worked at many of the fingerprinting clinics, distributing safety kits to children and their parents. Immersing herself in her job made her feel she was making a difference. She was determined to prevent a similar tragedy happening to another family.

At first, Barbara thought that if she mailed out enough posters, eventually Michael would be found. Even now, every Christmas she believes that Michael will come home; when Christmas comes and goes and it does not happen, she simply sets a new date for his return. A devout Catholic, her faith has sustained her through the years. She has lit many candles and prayed to many saints over the past twenty years, but despite the fact that her beloved grandson has not been found, she has never felt forsaken by or angry with God. Wherever Michael might be today, Barbara firmly believes that God is taking care of him.

Her dedication to child safety drove her to work hard at getting the Child Find safety program into the school system and, to that end, she has written numerous letters to politicians. She also writes "letters to the editor" on any topic about which she feels strongly, such as the HST recall, getting petitions signed and observing the ballot count.

Now in her mid-seventies, her daughter Karen describes her as "a gentle soul" whose strong beliefs have enabled her to get through the worst days. She still lives in the same house she and Harvey shared for years, just a few houses away from Bruce and Crystal.

Crystal's family was equally devastated by Michael's disappearance. It had a huge impact on Crystal's younger sister, Dorothy, who had flown out to be with her in 1991.

Jordan, the baby she was pregnant with at the time of Michael's abduction, was born on October 2, 1991. On May 4, 1995, she gave birth to her second son, Cody.

"My kids have grown up not knowing their cousin Michael, but they certainly know everything about him," says Dorothy. Her children also know how paranoid their mother was when they were small. Because of what had happened to Michael, Dorothy always found it hard to leave her children with anyone. Interviewing babysitters was also difficult for her because she didn't trust anyone. Fortunately, being a military wife meant she had a lot of close friends nearby who helped her.

She remembers that on one occasion her older son hid under a clothing rack in K-Mart and she couldn't find him. She began to panic and insisted they close the store down until he was found. Suddenly little Jordan appeared from his hiding place, saying, "Here I am, Mommy…" Dorothy had no idea how to react: hug him, scream at him or simply pass out with relief.

"I still get completely freaked out when I see children playing on their own without parental supervision; and also whenever I hear of another child that has gone missing. It can happen so quickly and I just can't believe how some people can be so reckless about watching their children and being responsible for them. They just do not think!"

Later in life, Jordan was diagnosed with attention deficit hyperactivity disorder (ADHD), about which Dorothy says, "This disorder might have developed in Jordan during my pregnancy when I was so stressed in that third month at the time of Michael's disappearance; but they have no way of knowing that for sure."

Dorothy has two special memories of Michael, one being trips she made with him to Toys "R" Us in Victoria whenever she visited, and the second from her own wedding in 1988. Michael, still quite small at the time, had been told that his aunt and new uncle had now become "Mr. and Mrs. Arseneault," but that was a name he could not pronounce. Instead he toddled around the reception telling all the guests that they were now called "Mr and Mrs. Ars." This, of course, caused great hilarity.

"I still can't believe this tragedy happened to my sister," states Dorothy. "It is so unfair…I was closest to Crystal growing up. I loved her very much and always looked up to her. She worked hard to get herself through college and I so admired that. She also always was very motherly to all her siblings. When she moved out I wanted to go with her; but I used to have weekend sleepovers at her apartment and I cherished those weekends. When I was fifteen I ran away from home once. She was married to Bruce by then, so they came to my rescue and took me in to live with them for about two years. Looking back now, I realize it must have been very challenging for them and a big adjustment because they were just newly married. I know I wasn't the easiest person to get along with, but we managed to keep it together and they were wonderful to me. I appreciate everything they both did for me."

Dorothy worries about her sister. "Sometimes it concerns me how she's always on the go so much. But I think that's what she must need in order to keep going. She is my everything and I love her to death, and don't know where I would be today without her influence. Her strength and stamina throughout her entire life must be how she has been able to cope with losing Michael. I honestly believe that Crystal is an angel from above that was sent to my parents for a reason. She's the strongest woman I know and I just wish now that there was more I could do for her."

Dorothy felt a close connection with her niece Caitlin since the moment she first held her when she arrived in Victoria after Michael's disappearance in 1991. Caitlin was just six months old.

"I hugged her so tightly that day," Dorothy says. "It seemed like we formed a special bond there and then…and to me she has always felt like the daughter I never had."

Approximately three years ago when Dorothy came to visit, Caitlin made an appointment for herself and her aunt to get tattoos as a lasting memory of Michael.

"She wanted to do it as some kind of closure, but it was very hard. I wanted to support her, so Caitlin, Crystal, me, my stepsister Yvonne and her daughter Sam, and my sister-in-law Kim, all went together. Caitlin had drawn a picture of what she wanted—the green ribbon for missing children with Michael Dunahee written through it. Mine was to be a picture of an angel with Michael's initials on it… Crystal sat beside Caitlin while she had hers done…Caitlin held my hand while I had mine done. It was all very emotional.

"Caitlin had told me that if she started crying, I was to look inside her purse where she had put something to give her strength and remind her why she was getting this done. When she started to cry, I immediately opened her purse and inside I found a framed picture of Caitlin and Michael on Caitlin's christening day. The picture was placed on the counter…and it seemed to give us the strength we needed…It was a very special day for all of us.

"I still pray that Michael will come home one day," she says. "I can't speak for the rest of my family, but I do know we all miss him terribly in our own ways. We all pull together for the run and the dance every year even though it is very hard on everyone as it brings back so many memories."

Steve Orcherton became a good friend of the Dunahees, working diligently on their behalf with both the Labour Council and Child Find. With a son the same age as Michael, Steve had always had a special connection to the Dunahee case and felt keenly the agony the Dunahees endured. He ultimately embarked on a career in politics and subsequently represented the electoral district of Victoria-Hillside in the Legislative Assembly from 1996 until 2001, sitting as a member of the New Democratic Party. He was defeated in the 2001 provincial election by Sheila Orr, the same candidate he had come up against in 1996. Orcherton again sought the New Democratic Party nomination in Victoria-Hillside in the 2005 election, but this time lost to Rob Fleming.

As executive director in the Victoria office of Child Find BC, he continues his work for missing children, in addition to supporting his wife, Peg Orcherton, who is a member of the Greater Victoria School Board.

Changes have abounded in the wider world since 1991. Technology has advanced light years. The internet has changed the way people learn, communicate and in many ways deal with the world at large. While in 1991, virtually no one had a personal computer, now we can carry one in our pocket and access and send information from anywhere to anywhere in seconds via smart phones—something else that did not exist in 1991.

Social networking, originally designed for easy communication among a small group of college students, has swept the world and wields enormous influence, even to the point of shaping political debate and influencing revolutions. Facebook, Twitter, YouTube—not even on anyone's radar in 1991—now play a vital role in worldwide communications.

The internet and social networking have become valuable tools in the search for missing children. Many police departments and provincial AMBER Alerts (although, interestingly, not BC) maintain Facebook pages. This makes it easy for anyone to pass along any information they may have with regard to any crime, especially those involving children. The police and missing children's organizations monitor various blogs for comments that may yield new leads. Many tips now originate that way, and the police examine every one that seems important. Certainly police officers in Victoria have investigated all information that came to their attention regarding Michael Dunahee, including social media commentary, and many remain under active investigation.

The Canadian Centre for Child Protection https://protectchildren.ca/app/en/ based in Winnipeg, is leading the way in using social media in many missing children cases. Their mission is to reduce the incidence of missing and sexually exploited children; educate the public on child personal safety and sexual exploitation; assist in the location of a missing child; and advocate for and increase the awareness about issues relating to missing and sexually exploited children. They have provided services for almost thirty years, starting as Child Find Manitoba and in 2006 forming the Canadian Centre for Child Protection.

There have also been great advances in the science of DNA with regard to testing procedures, DNA extraction from smaller samples and more sources, training, and expanded DNA databases. But unfortunately establishing a DNA databank for missing persons in Canada continues to be an unfulfilled dream.

On National Missing Children's Day in 2009, Crystal attended the RCMP headquarters in Vancouver to meet and support another mother, Judy Peterson, concerning the need for a DNA databank for missing persons' identification. Judy Peterson had been on a mission for nearly a decade lobbying the federal government for legislation that would match missing persons' DNA with any human remains found.

Her involvement came about as a result of the disappearance of her daughter, Lindsey Jill Nicholls, in 1993 when she was fourteen years old. It was believed at the time that Lindsey might have been hitchhiking, as she was last seen on a rural road outside Courtenay on Vancouver Island. After Lindsey had been missing for seven years, Peterson decided to enter her daughter's DNA to see if it matched the DNA of any unidentified human remains. She was amazed to discover that a databank as such did not exist in Canada. Although the software was available, it just had not been put into use.

"What if Lindsey had been murdered?" she stated. "What if her body was simply human remains somewhere? Canada has a crime scene and convicted offender DNA databank, but it is used only to identify criminals, not to link DNA from missing persons with unidentified remains."

Peterson had identified a gaping hole in existing DNA legislation, which could easily be filled by allowing the collection of DNA of all missing persons or their close relatives for the purpose of cross-referencing any DNA found at future crime scenes and unidentified human remains.

In 2003, then Solicitor General Wayne Easter told Peterson that legislation for such a databank was finally on the agenda. Following this, the Liberal MP for the Saanich-Gulf Islands, Gary Lunn, took up Peterson's cause by introducing a DNA Identification Act that year, naming it Lindsey's Law. By 2009 it still had not passed and Judy Peterson was becoming extremely frustrated.

However, working on Lindsey's Law had been therapeutic for her. She said that her quest for the DNA databank made her feel like she was still doing something to look for her daughter.

"It's been really good for me," she said. "I feel like I'm acknowledging Lindsey. Once this is in place, it may not find Lindsey, but we're going to find some kids and some parents will get closure. That's what I'm really looking forward to."

Passing Lindsey's Law would finally provide many grieving families with the closure they need for the victims of crime by identifying their loved one's remains, and it might even help to put the perpetrators of these crimes behind bars where they belong.

In December 2011, a new tip concerning the Lindsey Nicholls' case prompted the Comox Valley RCMP to search a rural property near the area of Royston on Vancouver Island. Unfortunately, they found nothing that would link the area to the Nicholls' case. Judy Peterson was aware of the search and knew that if that area had been a crime scene, a DNA databank of missing persons would have been vital in identifying any human remains found there.

To date Lindsey Nicholls, who would now be thirty-three years old, has never been found and Lindsey's Law has still not been passed. Peterson continues to push the federal government to pass the necessary legislation allowing investigators to collect DNA from missing persons or their close relatives. The petition on her website at www.lindseyslaw.com can be signed in support of this law.

Although the world has changed immeasurably since Michael vanished, with instant worldwide communication and many more technological tools to assist those fighting to recover missing children, child abduction has increased.

To anyone who has had a "feeling" about a possible sighting or suddenly recalls a long-forgotten memory, please do not hesitate to report your concerns to authorities. However obscure it may seem, a suspicious sighting or a strange memory may be the missing link in some family's missing child story. Perhaps even Michael's.

These days, with the technology literally at our fingertips, it is easy to pass along tips and concerns. If you feel you know something, please contact your local police or any one of the following organizations:

The Canadian Centre for Child Protection
www.protectchildren.ca
www.missingkids.ca

National Centre for Missing & Exploited Children
http://www.ncmec.org/

Child Find BC
www.childfind.bc

Michael Dunahee's own website
www.michaeldunahee.ca

Until a final answer is found, there is always hope, so nothing will ever be discounted.

CHAPTER 11

Never Stop Believing

Our hope is that one day we will have Michael back...simple as that.
—Crystal Dunahee, April 2011

The Dunahee family has never given up hope that one day they will find the answer to what happened on March 24 1991, and that Michael will be found. Everything they do to raise money for Child Find, is done to bring missing children home and reunite them with their parents. Nothing will deter them from their dedication to this cause.

What happened would have destroyed many families, but not the Dunahees. They have turned their heartbreak into hope, their torment into comfort for other families and protection for other children. They have been sustained on their painful journey by the knowledge of many happier endings and numerous success stories concerning other missing children, stories of children abducted and then found and returned to their families.

One such example was the abduction of Elizabeth Smart, a fourteen-year-old girl who was taken from her Salt Lake City, Utah home in 2002 and held captive in various locations for nine months. On March 12, 2003, she was found in Sandy, Utah, about eighteen miles from her home. She was wearing a disguise and in the company of Brian David Mitchell and Wanda Barzee, both of whom were indicted for her kidnapping and sexual assault. Although they were initially ruled unfit to stand trial, eventually Barzee was convicted in 2009 and sentenced to fifteen years in prison; Mitchell was convicted in 2010 and transferred to federal prison in August 2011 to begin serving a life sentence for his crimes.

Another incredible success story was that of eleven-year-old Jaycee Lee Dugard, kidnapped on June 10, 1991—the same year as Michael—in South Lake Tahoe, California. After being held captive for nineteen years by fifty-eight-year-old convicted sex offender Phillip Craig Garrido and his wife Nancy Garrido of Antioch, California, she was returned to her family in 2009.

Jaycee had been held in a concealed area behind Garrido's house, where she had been drugged and raped. She gave birth to two daughters, aged fifteen and eleven at the time of her rescue. Her discovery was the result of prompt action by people whose suspicions were aroused when Garrido visited the campus of the University of California at Berkeley on August 25, 2009, accompanied by two young girls (his daughters by Jaycee). The girls' extreme shyness attracted the attention of employees at the university and their concern triggered an investigation. Garrido was commanded to bring the girls to a parole office the next day. He complied, bringing Jaycee along with him. It was there that Jaycee Dugard was finally identified.

Today she is a remarkably strong young woman who has since written a book about her long ordeal. Her amazing story of survival in spite of all she endured, prove that determination and hope for all abductions should never falter.

A third incredible story that had a happy ending was the more recent abduction of three-year-old Kienan Hebert who disappeared from his home in Sparwood, British Columbia on Wednesday, September 7, 2011. At first it was believed that Kienan had been sleepwalking and wandered out of his house in the middle of the night and become lost. Later that same day, however, the RCMP issued an AMBER Alert. They suspected that sex offender Randall Hopley had abducted Kienan.

In 2008 Hopley had been sentenced to eighteen months in jail for a break-in in Sparwood when he tried to grab a ten-year-old boy. At the time he claimed he was attempting to return the child to his biological parents. Hopley also had eleven previous break-in convictions and had been convicted of sexual assault in 1985. However, at the time of Kienan's abduction, Hopley was out on probation and living in the Sparwood area, making him an obvious person of interest.

The Hebert family had to leave their home while the police investigation was carried out. A ground search was quickly organized and the Canadian military aerial team from Esquimalt brought in.

Kienan's father made an emotional plea via the media, speaking directly to the suspected kidnapper.

"If it's you, just bring Kienan back safely," he said. "Only God can deal with what we're dealing with. We can't deal with it; we're only human."

The RCMP also stated, "Nothing has been ruled out, but certainly we are considering foul play in this matter...but again, we remain hopeful and optimistic in thoughts with the family that we're going to have a positive outcome to this effort so far in locating the child unharmed and well."

Then, what seemed impossible happened—a miracle. Four days after the abduction, Kienan Hebert was returned to his home in the middle of the night, apparently in good health and unharmed. He was found curled up and sleeping peacefully in an armchair in the living room in the empty house. His alleged abductor had called the police to let them know where Kienan could be found.

The president of the Virginia-based National Center for Missing and Exploited Children said, "For an abductor to take a child in this manner—to penetrate the home, to come into the home, to take the child—and then return the child back to that home, is in many ways unprecedented. We've worked thousands of these cases and I don't remember one quite like it."

Although it is not uncommon for child sex offenders to release their victims alive, it is unheard of for a perpetrator to go to such great lengths to ensure a child's safe return, placing him securely back in his own home.

Credit for Kienan's safety can go, certainly in part, to the immediate and aggressive police response to his abduction, in addition to use of the conventional media, the internet and mobile phones alerting the public. The speed with which Randall Hopley was identified as a possible suspect was also a plus in this case. But did Kienan's father's emotional plea to Hopley also play a part? Was Hopley perhaps an abductor with a conscience?

The police continued to search for Hopley, and specifically asked him to turn himself in, saying, "We need to speak to you. It's very, very important that we speak to you, Randy. Our main concern now is for you to contact us."

The following Tuesday morning, a police dog found Hopley hiding in an abandoned cabin in an area where he had lived all his life, twenty kilometers (twelve miles) from Sparwood. He attempted to flee, with the police dog in pursuit, and was arrested a short time later. The next day, Hopley made his first court appearance, where the judge ordered that he undergo a psychiatric assessment to determine if he was fit to stand trial.

At a sentencing hearing in July 2012 the Crown asked that Hopley be designated a dangerous and long-term offender. Hopley, however, claimed he had taken Kienan as a protest against the justice system for his previous conviction for abducting the ten-year-old boy; he maintained he was innocent of that crime. He also stated he had never intended to harm Kienan and that he had already apologized to Kienan's father, who had forgiven him. Despite being continually pressed by the police as to why he had taken the little boy, he repeated it was a protest for being wrongfully accused earlier, and nothing more.

The Hebert family has since moved from Sparwood, and Hopley's fate is still in the hands of the court. The judge was not expected to rule until later, once the psychiatric assessment is complete.

Yet another happy-ending abduction case occurred in 1993 in Germany. Three-month-old Wilbert Grusser was kidnapped from his baby carriage at a municipal office in Dessau, an East German city. His mother, Susann Grusser, had left Wilbert alone for just a few moments under a staircase in the office building. She made repeated pleas on television begging the abductor to return her son to her. Many tips had come in, but all led nowhere.

Two years later, a particularly observant woman living in the city of Duisburg in the Ruhr Valley, was watching a TV program called *Without a Trace* on which there was a report on the case of the missing little boy. It reminded her that she had long been suspicious of her neighbour who had suddenly acquired a child in somewhat strange circumstances two years earlier. The neighbour claimed to have adopted the child, whom she called "Fabian," from a Polish woman. However, something simply did not add up, and the woman called the police. After comparing blood samples for genetic fingerprints of the child, he proved to be Wilbert Grusser. He was returned to his ecstatic rightful parents and his abductor taken into custody. The kidnapper had suffered a miscarriage shortly before she took Wilbert, and during the two years she kept him, she, thankfully, had treated him with the love of a mother. Miracles can and do happen.

It is a completely different scenario in the case of a parental abduction. That type of abduction rarely goes on for years. Most parental abduction cases are resolved within a fairly short time when either the police locate the absconding parent and the kidnapped child, or the fleeing parent voluntarily returns the child to the custodial parent without incident. Nonetheless, long-time parental abductions, such as the following case, can occur and can also have happy endings.

In December 2011, just such a case came to a startling conclusion in Victoria, British Columbia, when a father living in Toronto who had been searching for his abducted daughter for eighteen years finally learned her whereabouts, and also that the mother of his child had been arrested.

In 1993, Joe Chisholm and the mother of his daughter, who then went by the name of Patricia O'Bryne, had been in a long and difficult custody battle over their twenty-month-old daughter, Stephanie.[1] Their own relationship had deteriorated and they had separated, but they held joint custody of their baby. Then, on May 13, 1993, in the midst of the dispute and unpleasant legal hassles, Patricia took off with Stephanie and seemed to disappear off the face of the earth.

Through the years, Joe's search led him to Europe, where sightings had been reported in both the UK and Spain, and he chased down hundreds of tips across Canada, most of which he updated regularly on his Facebook page and on various family videos he released. Joe maintained he had been very close to finding his daughter on many occasions.

In 1999 an arrest had almost been made in England, but the mother left the place where she was spotted before the police arrived. Some time during the late 1990s and early 2000s, Joe pursued a tip that led him to Vancouver where he actually saw Patricia getting into a car near the Capilano Suspension Bridge. The authorities were notified immediately, but the elusive mother of his child once again disappeared.

---

[1] A pseudonym is used as the identity of the victim is protected by a court-ordered publication ban.

In the fall of 2011 a tip came in to the Alberta branch of The Missing Children's Society of Canada (MCSC) saying that Joe's daughter and his former partner were known to be living on Vancouver Island under assumed names. Joe was at first sceptical.

"I've heard tips like that so many times over the years that I know I can't just stop life. I just had to keep myself busy and wait it out. It's hard though, not to just try and get in there and control things, but I can't."

He decided to carry on with his life as a musician and financial adviser and being a father to his twenty-three-year-old son, Jesse (from a previous relationship), because he knew that the MCSC was working in conjunction with both the Toronto and Victoria police departments. He just hoped that it would all end satisfactorily.

What he did not know was that the Victoria police had been keeping surveillance on a fifty-three-year-old woman well known in Victoria under an assumed name. There was concern that she might have been a flight risk if she knew she was being watched. But on Thursday, December 1, 2011, Patricia O'Bryne was arrested without incident at her home. Her daughter, Stephanie, who also had been going by a different name, was not in town at the time as she was attending university in Ontario. At the same time that her mother was being arrested, police in Ontario were telling Stephanie the news and helping her to absorb the shock of learning her true identity. It was not known exactly what her mother had told her through the years about their past or her father.

This case, although ending happily for a distraught father who had searched for almost two decades, is also in many ways a tragedy for both his daughter and ex-partner. Patricia O'Bryne and her daughter were well respected in Victoria. O'Bryne, under her assumed name, which is now under a publication ban, held a provincial government communications job and had always been very active in her daughter's school, serving as both vice-president and president of the parent advisory council (PAC). The principal at Victoria High School, from where Stephanie graduated in 2009 as an honours student and co-valedictorian, was shocked by the news, as were many friends of both mother and daughter. Stephanie was also a keen athlete, volunteered in her community and had recently travelled to Africa before attending university. Her peers admired her, stating, "She has a great sense of social justice."

Stephanie now had to face the fact that her mother had committed a crime, and that she had a father and another family, about which she had had no knowledge. It would be an enormous amount for a young person to digest.

This particular parental abduction case was the longest on record in Canada by the missing children's services at the Canadian Centre for Child Protection. On December 2, 2011, the executive director of MCSC issued a press release stating, "Seeing this case come to a close is incredibly exciting and moving for us. Our investigators have been working on this case, assisting law enforcement and Stephanie's father, for nearly two decades. This is one of the longest-term cases we have on file, and it renews our hope and determination for our many other cases."

But how had Stephanie managed to attend both Central Middle School and Victoria High School without the requisite pieces of official identification needed for students to enroll? The school district apparently did hold a copy of a long version of a valid birth certificate for her, showing her birth date as February 18, 1992 in Toronto. Her mother's name was listed, but the space for father was left blank. This document had been issued on June 3, 1996. There was also a copy of a Canadian passport for her, issued in December 2009, showing the same birth date.

This raises the question: How can someone obtain false identification so easily? In light of this parental abduction case, the Canadian Children's Rights Council is pressing for a change in both federal and provincial laws and regulations. The council would like to see paternity tests carried out at birth so that both parents are identified immediately. This would certainly help to eliminate paternal and identity fraud at a later date.

At present, regulations are often ignored even though the Vital Statistics Act in Ontario, for example, requires that the names on the statement of live birth forms should be verified. In Ontario currently, at least 5 percent of all birth registrations have no father listed on the birth certificate, and no one verifies the information given on the form. Anyone can submit a form and create a new identity for a child; all that needs to be stated is that it was a home birth and there is a witness name on the form. The current system makes it far too easy for identity theft. It is a very dangerous situation for abducted children.

As the days went by following the arrest of Patricia O'Bryne, other things came to light. It was learned that when Stephanie was informed of this news she was not totally surprised. Apparently some things had taken place between her and her mother over the previous two years which made her suspect something was not quite right. She was not, therefore, completely shocked to hear from the police.

It was also learned, after her initial appearance in court and bail was denied, that O'Bryne might face additional charges, as would some of her family members and friends. It was obvious that she could not have carried out this charade for eighteen years without help from others who may have aided and abetted her along the way. It was thought that there could be at least five family members involved, plus a neighbour.

She had allegedly spent time in Ireland. School records there showed Stephanie had attended a primary school, St. Mary's National School in Waterpark, Carrigaline, a small community of some 11,000 residents approximately 112 kilometers (seventy miles) south of County Cork. So, Patricia O'Bryne obviously had contacts to help her live undercover not only in Canada, but also in Europe.

Eventually Patricia O'Bryne was granted bail and allowed to return to Victoria temporarily until her case is heard in Toronto, at which time her side of the story will undoubtedly also be heard.

As of mid 2012, Joe Chisholm is waiting for his daughter to approach him. He has no wish to force himself and other family members on her too soon, and wants to allow her time to digest everything first.

Wendy Christensen, manager of investigation for MCSC, and a former member of the RCMP, said, "Now that Stephanie has been located, there will be a long road of healing and challenges for the family. It is our hope that people will respect the privacy of the family at this emotional time and their difficult journey ahead. Since Stephanie's disappearance, we have actively investigated any and all tips which have come into our office and worked hand-in-hand with law enforcement to ensure that they were always provided with our investigative findings. In this particular case, MCSC received a tip which, after further investigation, we felt confident would bring much needed closure to Stephanie's disappearance. As is our practice, we forward this information to the Toronto Police Service for further investigation. Over the past twenty-five years, North Americans have contacted MCSC with information which, for their own reasons, they chose not to bring to the attention of law enforcement. This investigation is an example of what can be accomplished when we all work together to ensure that our primary objective of locating missing children is met.

"I can't tell you how many law enforcement officers and police agencies in North America and other countries have been involved in this investigation over the years—there have been many. We are humbled by their efforts and unwavering dedication. To the members of the Toronto Police Service, and to law enforcement agencies in BC who assisted Toronto Police in this portion of the investigation, we thank you for everything you have done. It is through partnerships such as this that we make the world of anyone who chooses to take a child a very small place. To each and every individual who has called MCSC and law enforcement agencies with information over the past eighteen years, we thank you most of all as, without you, none of this would be possible."

The particular story of Patricia O'Bryne and her daughter Stephanie, although a completely different type of abduction, brought Michael Dunahee's case to the forefront once again by giving renewed hope to the family and to police investigators.

If someone could live a totally different life with a new identity for eighteen years, could not something similar have happened to Michael for over twenty years? It also demonstrates that whoever abducted Michael, for whatever purpose, must have had assistance and there could indeed still be others who know what happened to Michael—perhaps even where he is today.

Deputy Chief John Ducker of the Victoria Police Department stated, "Because of this latest child abduction case—and happening right here in Victoria—we are all thinking of the Dunahee case again, and we are certainly still working each and every day to bring closure to that particular two-decade old mystery."

The executive director of MCSC added to that: "This is an important day for our organization, which just marked twenty-five years in the search for missing children. And this is an important day for our searching families. It proves that no matter what, if a child has been missing for eighteen minutes or eighteen years, we will never give up the search."

These success stories with happy endings continue to inspire families of missing children to never give up hope. Anything is possible.

CHAPTER 12

A Letter to Michael

Michael, we now need a miracle to happen.

—Valerie Green, author

With the preceding success stories in mind, the following letter is written to Crystal and Bruce's missing son.

Dear Michael:

If, by some miracle, you are reading this letter, it is important that you know and understand your true roots and the story of what happened to you back in March of 1991. This book has told you that story.

Your real parents are Bruce and Crystal Dunahee, and they are two of the bravest people imaginable. They have suffered the greatest tragedy any parent will ever know, the loss of a child, and yet they have valiantly tried to make a new life without you. It was not how they planned their future. Not only did you disappear from their lives, they also have no idea what happened to you or who took you that day. They have been deprived of fully grieving for you because there is no answer to the mystery and no conclusion to this story.

Nonetheless, they have never given up hope that one day you will be found, and to this end they have dedicated their lives to numerous ways of helping to find other missing children. Although they were unable to find you, their own beloved son, they have assisted in returning other children to their families and in keeping other children safe. That takes enormous courage.

They hope that the things that were taught to you in the first four and a half years of your life have somehow remained with you in your sub-conscious. If, today, you are a young man in your mid-twenties, maybe you occasionally have a flashback to another time and to other faces. Maybe this book will resurrect those vague memories and make you wonder about those deep-rooted recollections and flashbacks and you will want to explore those feelings and understand what they all mean.

Perhaps you might recall an old favourite toy; a favourite breakfast cereal; a crying baby who was your sister, Caitlin; a ceremony in a church when your baby sister was christened; playing baseball with your real dad; going with your dad to Fleming Beach to watch the fishing boats coming in; being babysat by a fun-loving aunt and visiting Toys "R" Us with another aunt; going fishing with a man who was your granddad; playing with Blue, your Aunt Karen's dog; listening to your real mother telling you a bedtime story and tucking you in at night; cuddling up with Dad on the couch.

Hold on to those fleeting memory flashes, Michael, because they are real. Those things actually happened.

For all the years since you have been gone, your parents have kept the same telephone number. In 1991, as a small boy of four and a half, you knew that number and could proudly recite it. Since then an area code—250—has been added in front of the number. If that telephone number has been retained somewhere in your sub-conscious, you can still dial it today. Just add the 250 area code and your real parents will be there—waiting for your call, anxious to hear your voice. Or, you can telephone any of the numbers at the beginning of this book or in the appendices at the end, and explain all your concerns and whom you think you might be.

Your parents' love and faith have never diminished in over twenty years. Your mother's work with Child Find BC makes her realize that she and your dad are by no means alone in their grief for a lost child. There are far too many similar situations around the world—parents who are desperately waiting for answers to a mystery that no amount of police investigation has been able to solve. Parents need answers. They need to know what happened.

If you are still out there somewhere, Michael, today you will have a completely different identity and maybe even a different appearance from the latest age-enhanced photograph in this book—but you are still **you.** You are still Michael Wayne Dunahee (remember how you never wanted to be called Mike of Mikey), son of Crystal and Bruce, brother of Caitlin, and you are loved and missed by a family who were robbed of the chance of seeing you grow into a young man. Nothing can ever replace all those lost years for them, but just to see you again and to know you are well and happy is a hope they have never lost.

Only your abductor or abductors know the truth about your disappearance that day. They have kept that appalling secret for over two decades and it is now time to break the silence. An answer is well overdue. All those who love you need to know, so it is never too late for that person or persons to disclose the truth. The waiting has gone on for far too long. We now need a miracle to happen.

We need to know what happened on that morning in March of 1991 when you vanished from our lives. Meanwhile, we will never lose hope.

Michael, we love you.

(Signed): The Dunahee Family, the Victoria Police Department, Child Find BC and the author of this book.

Conclusion

Never, ever give up on your dreams.

—Betty Fox, mother of Canadian hero Terry Fox

Today British Columbia's capital city is a popular tourist destination. Victoria's façade displays a pleasant place to visit and to live. For many people, what occurred back in 1991 has been lost in the sands of time. In reality, only those close to the criminal act of Michael Dunahee's abduction continue to bear the real pain. But the community that was shocked beyond belief because of a missing little boy and an act that compelled the entire population to come together for a common cause could no longer hold the innocent belief that "those things don't happen here."

Unlike the terror that gripped the Metro Vancouver region in 1980–81 when serial killer Clifford Olsen murdered his young victims, the disappearance of Michael Dunahee ten years later touched everyone in a totally different way. He was the first such missing-child case in Victoria—a rare stranger abduction—and, for that reason he became everyone's child back in 1991 and the poster child for missing children everywhere.

Because Michael was so young and in the care of his parents when he was snatched—in mere seconds—his abduction became the turning point for every mother and father. Parents became more vigilant. There were predators out there and children needed to be protected from them. Children were no longer allowed to walk to school alone or to play unsupervised outside. It became very important to thoroughly screen anyone who would be supervising or caring for children. But even with this hard-won awareness and diligence children continue to go missing every day. It has become a shocking fact of life as we hear of more cases around the world.

As a result, in protecting our children—our most vulnerable human beings—children who grew up in the 1990s and into the twenty-first century have lost a valuable part of childhood: the thrill of becoming independent and of growing into maturity with confidence.

And sadly, some predators are already known to the child—and trusted by them—so it becomes difficult for children to determine who will harm them and who will not. Who should they trust? Childhood in our modern age sometimes seems to be too complex even for adults, let alone children.

During the years 2000 and 2001 there were ninety police reports across Canada initially classified as stranger abductions; however, many of those "strangers" were in fact relatives, friends or acquaintances. With a parental abduction, the child's threat is only from one of the parents, whereas with a stranger abduction, the threat is multifarious and can cover a diversified group of people.

Thankfully, stranger abduction in Canada is rare; but when it does happen it shocks us all. And, because of hyped media releases that describe these kidnappings in detail, paranoia is heightened. Parents everywhere are naturally concerned for the safety of their children; hopefully the many tips provided in the appendices of this book will answer some of their concerns and give them the information they need.

The purpose of this book has not been necessarily to try and solve the mystery of Michael Dunahee's disappearance—although that would be a wonderful outcome indeed if it were to happen. His story, like those of so many other missing children, should not be sensationalized by dramatic media exposure or by this book. What happened to Michael is a tragedy of the worst kind and, hopefully, has been presented in that way in the foregoing text. The truth behind all cases of missing or abducted children is far more painful than any exaggerated or embellished prose. The foremost reason for telling Michael's story is to bring into focus the plight of missing and exploited children and their families. Some of these children are runaways; some are the innocent victims of parental abduction; some were abducted by strangers.

A secondary purpose is to show how child abduction such as

Michael's, which has provided no answers for over twenty years, affects and changes a family. For the Dunahees this has meant working hard at life to keep their family together so that Michael had a place to come home to, helping others through similar ordeals by devoting themselves to the cause, and simply keeping their own hope alive by any and all means, in spite of the passage of time with no resolution.

Since 1991, the world has become familiar with the names of many missing children, some of which have been mentioned in this story. Unfortunately several of those stories ended tragically, but there have been many others that had positive endings. Those are the ones that give hope to families such as the Dunahees.

In 1991, police investigation standards were vastly different from what they are today, and a missing child investigation in Victoria was something completely new. Nonetheless, the Victoria police department, the military, the RCMP, search and rescue, the FBI Behavioral Science Unit, Child Find and the Missing Children's Society, as well as the police departments of the municipalities of Oak Bay, Esquimalt and Saanich, all joined forces in a common cause doing the best they could with the tools available at that time. With today's technology, they would probably have had more to work with. For one thing, the car park that day would have been full of people with cell phones with cameras. Something might have been seen and caught on someone's phone. A predator would have been more visible. Possibly there would have been a more reliable witness.

Even so, would they have found the answer to what occurred that day? Would Michael now be home where he belongs? It is something we will never know.

One Victoria police officer currently involved in Michael's abduction keeps the following quote in mind at all times, believing passionately that it pertains to *every* missing persons case: "When you have eliminated the impossible, whatever remains, **however improbable**, must be truth."[1] It is his constant reminder to keep an open mind to every possibility. He, as have so many others who worked this case over the past twenty-one years, remains strongly focused on eliminating all impossibilities. One day when that is done, what is left will surely be the truth.

---

[1] From *The Sign of Four* by Sir Arthur Conan Doyle.

Michael was one of Victoria's own, and because there was no evidence to prove otherwise, everyone wanted to believe that his story would end happily and he would be safely returned to his family. Even after two decades that hope is still paramount. No one attached to this story has ever stopped believing and no one ever should. Miracles happen all the time.

Maybe, without realizing it, you have that answer. Perhaps, as another police officer said at the very beginning of the search, we are still only "a connection or two away from the truth."

And then, finally, this story will have an ending.

Author's Last Word

As I write this, fall is on its way and another Christmas will soon be upon us, the time when families celebrate being together.

In the Dunahee family, a grandmother will once again pin her hopes on this significant Christmas date as the time when she believes her grandson will be home with his family. If that does not happen, the family will sit down to dinner once more with one empty place at the table, with a mother and father thinking of their little boy who, if he is still alive somewhere in the world, is now a grown man they don't even know; a sister imagining what it might have been like to have a big brother sitting beside her, perhaps teasing her; an aunt forcing laughter to lighten the mood; grandparents who have been cheated from knowing their grandchild.

Similar scenarios take place in thousands of homes around the world where an abducted child or a missing person is absent from the family table and their whereabouts are not known. These are stories without endings or closure of any kind—good or bad.

Although Michael's story, like all those others, does not have an ending yet, my work on telling it in book form has now reached a closure of sorts. For me, it is now a time for reflection; and in this contemplation I am reminded again of one thing. Every book I have written started out with just a small grain of information, which quickly seemed to take on a life of its own. That tiny seed of an idea invariably grew into a larger idea that, in turn, became an outline for a story and then finally a full body of work. The writing journey for each of those books can be compared to a small acorn slowly growing into a giant oak. And each one of those book "journeys" has always somehow seemed to have its own inner story, thereby turning into a narrative within the story itself. The writing of *Vanished* was no exception.

In 1991, like everyone else living in Victoria, I was touched beyond measure by Michael Dunahee's disappearance. As a mother, I could not imagine anything more horrendous than having one of my children taken from me.

My own two children were a few years older than Michael and Caitlin, but nevertheless I have always felt a strong connection with the Dunahee children. Like Michael and Caitlin, my children, Matthew and Kate, were four years apart in age. My son Matt has always called his younger sister "Caitlin," for reasons he alone knows. Michael's birthday is May 12, one day before mine; Catlin's birthday is September 7, one day after my mother's. Just coincidences maybe, but those associations have always had a special meaning for me.

I clearly remember the years when as a family we went to watch Matt play soccer and Kate wanted to play on nearby playgrounds. A somewhat adventurous little girl, we always told her to "stay within sight," but even with precautions in place it could well have been our daughter who was snatched in a split second when we looked the other way for just a moment. As parents, we were certainly not alone in those thoughts.

Perhaps for that reason, Michael's story has haunted me through the years, and on many occasions I felt the need to write about it. Many times I considered doing an article, and I often even thought about doing a book, but it never seemed quite the right time, either in my own life or for me to approach the Dunahee family for their permission to write about Michael's story. I reasoned that it might never be the right time for them either. Surely they'd had more than enough of being exposed to the media. Did they really need one more person probing into their lives and exposing their pain?

Then, in early 2011, while working on a completely different book—*Mysterious British Columbia,* a collection of mysteries set in British Columbia—it was suggested to me that I should include a chapter on the Michael Dunahee disappearance. Michael's story had been, and still was, such a high profile case that it definitely should not be omitted. It was after all one of the most horrifying, unsolved mysteries that British Columbia has ever known. This perhaps was the final push that I had needed to re-think the idea of writing a full-length book, in addition to the chapter that I included in *Mysterious British Columbia.*

So, with renewed motivation, I spoke to someone who had a connection to Crystal Dunahee through their mutual workplace, after which I then contacted Crystal to set up a meeting in July 2011. From that first contact and from many meetings since, plus talking with other family members, family friends, Child Find BC and the Victoria police, Michael's story has finally evolved into this book.

As I began to make contact with those who were involved in the story, almost everything seemed to fall into place with ease, as though meant to be. Even the few setbacks and obstacles in the writing process were eventually overcome.

Many times I asked myself, "How is this happening so effortlessly? Was it meant that this book should be written at this particular time? Could there be an underlying motive for its existence; and could that motive lead us to the answer we are all seeking?"

So, if Michael himself should ever read this book, thereby discovering his true identity, I would finally have found the true purpose of writing *Vanished*—and therein would exist the very ultimate "story within a story" and the greatest possible outcome to this journey.

I make no apology for my book being presented in this optimistic light, for that is the way the Dunahee family still sees things—and I agree. In the meantime, I also will never stop believing or keeping the hope alive as we all wait for the answers we need or, best of all, for that empty place at the Christmas table to be filled once again.

—VALERIE GREEN
Victoria, BC
Fall 2012

Appendix I
AMBER Alert System and GPS

AMBER Alert

AMBER Alert is a child abduction alert bulletin that was developed in the US and since has been adopted by many countries. AMBER is an acronym for "America's Missing: Broadcasting Emergency Response"; however it was originally named for Amber Hagerman, a nine-year-old who was abducted outside her home in Arlington, Texas on January 13, 1996, and subsequently murdered.

In Canada, every province has an AMBER Alert program for the most serious, time-critical abductions. Local police partner with media broadcasting agencies to solicit help from the public to locate the missing child. The alerts are also issued via e-mail, electronic traffic-condition signs and other LED billboards, and through wireless device text messages.

The decision to declare an AMBER Alert is made by each police department handling the investigation, and each province has its own activation criteria; however in general, the following guidelines are used:

- Law enforcement must confirm that an abduction has taken place. This is essential when determining the level of risk to the child. Stranger abductions are the most dangerous and thus are the primary impetus for an AMBER Alert.
- The child should be at risk of serious injury or death.
- The law enforcement agency must have enough information to believe that an immediate broadcast to

the public will enhance their efforts to locate the child and apprehend the suspect. There must be sufficient descriptive information of child, captor, or captor's vehicle to issue an alert. Issuing alerts without significant information that abduction has occurred could lead to abuse of the system and ultimately weaken its effectiveness.

- Age of Child: Most areas across North America adopt the "17 years of age or younger" standard, but the age taken can vary from place to place.

Unfortunately, had the AMBER Alert system been in existence in 1991, it would not have helped Michael's case, as the parameters needed for it to work were simply not there: no witness to his abduction, no licence plate number available.

On May 26 2010, Canada's wireless telecommunications industry, in partnership with the Royal Canadian Mounted Police (RCMP) the Ontario Provincial Police and AMBER Alert agencies across the country, introduced Wireless AMBER Alerts. This new initiative enables customers of most Canadian wireless services to opt-in to receive free AMBER Alerts as text messages on their cell phones.

The completely free Wireless AMBER Alerts program is now available to cell phone users in all ten provinces in Canada. Subscribing is easy and can be done either online at www.WirelessAMBER.ca or directly from your wireless device as follows:

Subscribing online at www.WirelessAmber.ca
1. Enter your 10-digit mobile number, including area code and click Submit.
2. You will then receive a text message on your mobile phone with a four-letter validation PIN code. Enter the PIN online and click Submit.
3. The Subscription page appears, with your home province or territory defaulted. Here you have the ability to check or uncheck additional provinces that you wish to subscribe to.
4. To modify your subscription at any time to add or . remove a province(s) or territory, just visit www.WirelessAMBER.ca and enter your 10-digit mobile

number and confirm using the four-letter validation PIN code. You will then be presented with a page where you have the option to update your selected provinces or territories. To unsubscribe from your current subscription, simply unselect all checkboxes. Alternatively, you can send the keyword STOP to 26237 (AMBER) at any time from your mobile phone.

Subscribing with your wireless device:
Most customers can follow these instructions to subscribe to Wireless AMBER Alerts directly from their wireless device.

1. Text the keyword AMBER to 26237 (AMBER).
2. You will be asked whether you would like to receive alerts in English or in French. Reply with either EN or FR.
3. You will receive a link to a mobile site where your home province or territory is defaulted. For example, if you sign up using a mobile phone number with a 416 area code, you will automatically be signed up to receive Wireless AMBER Alerts originating from Ontario.
4. To add or remove a province(s) or territory, simply text AMBER to 26237 (AMBER), and then follow the link to the mobile site to your previously saved settings. To unsubscribe, text the keyword STOP to 26237 (AMBER) at any time.

Most Canadian carriers are participating in this program. A complete list is available at www.wirelessamber.ca/partners.html

GPS

GPS tracking devices can now be used to locate missing children. These devices come in several different types; not all are appropriate for use by parents and the more high-tech devices are mainly for use by law enforcement. If a parent decides to invest in a child-tracking device, it is best to choose one that can be used for a variety of applications, both indoors and outdoors.

One model is appropriate for tracking teens and can track the car he or she is driving. Once installed, it can give location and speed information. Real time alerts are available on some models and enable a parent to tell if their child is walking or in a vehicle and exactly where the teen is located.

Most GPS tracking devices use the internet to report the child's location and will send out alerts via the company's website. Messages can also be sent to the myriad and growing number of smart phones available today. Some devices can even allow parents to track their children in 3D using Google Earth or Microsoft Virtual Earth. Updates can be given as often as every fifteen seconds if desired.

Prices for these tracking devices range from $150 to $600 and the monthly service fees vary from $15 to $20. Devices with more advanced features can cost up to as much as $69 per month. For many parents, the sense of security that comes from having a GPS child-tracking device far outweighs the cost. Statistics show that the number of missing persons has greatly increased in the past twenty years; almost 80 percent are juveniles. With a GPS tracking device and monitoring systems designed for child tracking, parents will have the assurance that their child's location is known at all times.

Law officials searching for a missing person can implement GPS tracking systems to track cell phones and other portable devices such as a mobile watch and can detect the exact location of that person, as long as the tracking device is activated and being carried by the missing person.

Appendix II
Safety Tips from Child Find
Fingerprinting Clinics; Tips for Tots; Tips for Schoolchildren; Tips for Teens; Cybersafe; Street Proof; Rules for Children of All Ages; Tips for Parents; What to Do if You See a Missing Child

Fingerprinting

Child Find offers free fingerprinting for children (accompanied by a parent or legal guardian) at their offices across the country. The fingerprints are recorded in an ID booklet "All About Me" which contains a detailed questionnaire about the child for the parent to complete and keep in a safe place in case their child should ever be reported missing. The questionnaire includes medical and dental history, a list of immediate family, friends and relatives, educational history, physical and mental characteristics and traits. Police also hold actual DNA samples from a missing child in their files; samples can be taken from clothing, a hairbrush, a comb or a toothbrush. Unfortunately, however, there is as yet no completed database on missing children in Canada to enable any found remains of a deceased person to be cross-referenced to a missing person.

The ID booklet presents itself as an invaluable document of needed information.

Tips for Tots

Use these Tips for Tots to explain these safety rules to children who are too young to read. It is important that you not frighten your child, but with repetition, try to teach the following:

- Never get into a car with a stranger.
- Always play with a friend—BE A BUDDY.

- Do not take presents from strangers.
- If a car pulls up where you are playing, BACK AWAY and run either home or to a safe or "Block Parent" house.[1]
- Never go anywhere without permission.
- Practice dialing your phone number, including your area code.
- Never open the door if you are home alone and dial 911 if you are frightened. Know your home address.
- Do not let anyone touch you in a way that makes you feel nervous. SAY "NO" AND GO.
- Select a code word. Make it simple and repeat it often. Tell your child he or she is only to go with someone who knows the code word (such as a parent or trusted family member).
- Assure your child of your love and that he or she will not be blamed if he or she tells the truth.
- It is sometimes a better learning experience if you teach several children at the same time. Repeat the rules often, as young children have a short memory span. Be sure to assure your child of your love and approval.
- If an adult asks you for help, say "NO" and tell your parents or teacher. Adults should ask adults for help, not children.

Tips for School Children

- Always tell your parents where you will be.
- Travel in groups or with a buddy; there is safety in numbers.
- If you see someone hanging around the schoolyard or the park, tell your teacher or parent. Learn to give a good description—is the person tall or short, dark or light skinned, eye and hair colour; and if he or she is in a vehicle—the make and model of the car and the license plate number.
- Do not accept job offers, rides or gifts from any stranger.

[1] The Block Parent Program of Canada works with educators and police to make communities safer for children, teens and seniors. www.blockparent. ca/

Even if you know the person, do not go with him or her unless you tell your parents first.

- Do not take dares to go to remote places.
- It is no fun to run away from home. Nothing is so terrible that you cannot tell your parents or another trusted adult.
- Do not answer the door when you are home alone. Do not tell people that you will be alone.
- If someone persists in calling or trying to get in, call the police at once.
- Do not go up to people who are asking for directions from a vehicle: step back and tell them you do not know and walk away quickly. Adults should not be asking children for directions.
- If someone touches you in a way that feels bad, YELL AND TELL. It is your body and nobody has the right to make you feel bad. TELL your parents, teacher or someone else you trust.
- Do not go with strangers, even if they are dressed like a policeman or if they promise you such things as a movie career. Talk with your parents first.

Tips for Teens

- DO NOT RUN AWAY FROM HOME. If things are impossible at home, speak to your teacher or your counsellor about it. They will help you. TALK IT OVER WITH A FRIEND WHO CARES. If you feel you have no friends that can help, find a crisis centre in your town. They are there to help, not judge. Kids Help Phone[1] is available 24/7. Call 1-800-668-6868.
- Be careful of offers of friendship from strangers. When you are lonely and unhappy, it is easier to be misled by signs of affection from strangers.
- Do not accept job offers that seem too good to be true. Use legitimate channels, such as student placement offices, for your part-time jobs. Check all references.

---

[1] KidsHelpPhone.ca is a free, anonymous and confidential phone and on-line professional counselling service for big or small concerns.

- Do not accept offers to take your photograph and make you famous. Report such offers at home or to police.
- Do not get into cars with strangers for any reason or get near enough to occupied vehicles to be grabbed. DO NOT HITCHHIKE.
- Travel in a group or with a friend.
- Do not go into remote areas at night.
- Do not take dares to do foolish things.
- Tell your parents where you are going to be and let them know when your plans change.
- Do not baby-sit in a home for people you do not know.
- If anyone touches you in a way that makes you uncomfortable—TELL.
- Report any incident of attempted molestation or if someone is hanging around your school or recreation areas. Learn to give a good description.
- Remember, IT IS NOT YOUR FAULT if someone has bothered you, so do not be afraid to tell. Doing so can protect you and others.
- Do not linger alone in unsupervised areas—leave with your friends.
- Do not open the door to strangers and do not tell people you are alone.
- Do not accept offers of drink, cigarettes or drugs.
- A date doesn't give someone the right to touch you or be physically demanding. Your body belongs to you. You have the right to say "NO."

Cybersafe

- Establish rules for internet use with your parents or another adult, including when you can go online, for how long and what activities you can do online. Post your rules next to your computer for easy reference.
- Keep the computer in a common space, like the family room or den.
- Don't share your password with anyone else, and never give out the following information: your real name, address (including your town or city), age, school, phone number or other personal information.

- Check with your parents before signing up for something online, or giving out a credit card number.
- Never send a photograph of yourself to someone in email unless your parents say it's okay.
- Check with your parents or another adult you trust before going into a chat room. Different chat rooms have different rules and attract different kinds of people. You and your parents will want to make sure it's an appropriate place for you.
- Never agree to meet someone you met on the internet in person without your parents' permission. Never meet anyone you met online alone, or in an isolated place. Meet in a public place, and go with your parents or an adult you trust.
- When you are online, what you do is up to you. Don't do anything that makes you uncomfortable. Trust your instincts.
- If someone online asks you too many personal questions, be suspicious and stop talking with them.
- Always remember that people online may not be who they say they are. Treat everyone online as if they were strangers.
- Be careful when someone offers you something for free, like gifts or money. Decline the offer and tell your parents.
- If you receive unwanted, offensive, mean, threatening, or harassing email, do not respond to it—tell your parents or another adult right away.
- If something you see or read online makes you uncomfortable, leave the site. Tell a parent or teacher right away.
- Treat other people as you'd like to be treated. Never use bad language or send mean messages online.
- Remember: not everything you read on the internet is true.
- The "off" button is always there. Use it if you need to. You don't have to stay online.

Cybertip.ca: Every year thousands of children are exploited on the internet. Through the hard work and commitment of Child Find Manitoba, in partnership with several donors and the government, cybertip.ca has been created to handle tips from individuals reporting the online sexual exploitation of children. If you have information regarding incidents of child pornography, luring, child sex tourism or child prostitution we would encourage you to visit this site.

The information you provide is made available to law enforcement to investigate and review. All reports are contained in a highly secure environment.

Street Proof

- Teach your child his/her full name, address and phone number.
- Explain how to use the telephone, area codes, collect calls, pay phones.
- Define a stranger; a person seen daily is still a stranger.
- Tell your children it's best to travel in groups and stay away from isolated areas.
- Instruct your children to report any suspicious people or incidents to you.
- Teach children to run, scream, yell, kick and fight if threatened by a stranger.
- No one has the right to touch your children in a way that makes them feel uncomfortable.
- Tell your children that when they are home alone, not to let people know they are by themselves. They should call for Mom even if she's not at home.

Rules for Children of all Ages

1. Before I go anywhere, I always check first with my parents or the person in charge. I tell them where I am going, how I will get there, who will be going with me, and when I'll be back.
2. I check first for permission from my parents before getting into a car or leaving with anyone—even someone I know. I check first before changing plans or accepting money or gifts without my parents' knowledge.

3. I will tell my parents or the authorities if someone tries to give me drugs.
4. It is safer for me to be with other people when going places or playing outside. I always use the "buddy system."
5. I say "NO" if someone tries to touch me in ways that make me feel frightened, uncomfortable, or confused. Then I go and tell a grown-up I trust what happened.
6. I know it is not my fault if someone touches me in a way that is not okay. I don't have to keep secrets about those touches.
7. I trust my feelings and talk to grown-ups about problems that are too big for me to handle on my own. A lot of people care about me and will listen and believe me. I am not alone.
8. It is never too late to ask for help. I can keep asking until I get the help I need.
9. I am a special person, and I deserve to feel safe. My rules are:
   • Check first.
   • Use the "Buddy System."
   • Say no, then go and tell.
   • Listen to my feelings, and talk with grown-ups I trust about my problems and concerns.

Tips for Parents: Caution
• Never leave a child unattended in a vehicle.
• Keep your child in sight when at all possible or know who your child is with and where.
• Be sure your child's school or daycare centre will not release him to anyone but you or someone designated by you.
• Set a code word with your child to be used as a signal if you send an unfamiliar adult to pick him up.
• Know your child's routes to school, their friend's house or favourite places.
• Be extremely cautious and thorough when selecting babysitters, preschools and daycares. Check references; know the person.

- Keep a copy of your child's fingerprints and be able to locate dental records. Take photographs every year (four times annually for children under two).
- Don't buy items with your child's name on them, such as T-shirts or lunch boxes. Children will respond more readily to a stranger if they are addressed by name.

A missing child is everyone's responsibility, so if you think you have seen a missing child, here is what you should do:

1. Contact your local authorities.
2. Contact Child Find 1-800-387-7962
3. NEVER confront the situation yourself. Allow the proper authorities to do that for you.
4. Be quietly observant. Take down any license numbers that may be pertinent. Write down descriptions of the people who the child was with. Also, record the colour of the child's hair, eyes and other distinguishing characteristics, if you are close enough to see them.

Although you may not be sure that the child you have seen is in fact one of the faces in the missing children's publication, it is always better to be wrong than to have passed up an opportunity to bring that child home. Any information you provide will be kept confidential if desired.

• • •

All the above information is taken from the website
of Child Find BC, with their permission.

Appendix III
National Child Exploitation Co-ordination Centre

The National Child Exploitation Coordination Centre (NCECC) is part of the Canadian Police Centre for Missing and Exploited Children (CPCMEC), which encompasses both the NCECC and the National Missing Children Services (NMCS).

The NCECC was established in 2004 as the law enforcement component of Canada's National Strategy to Protect Children from Sexual Exploitation on the internet. The Centre was created in response to the recognition that the internet was being more frequently used to facilitate sexual exploitation crimes against children, including the exchange of child sexual abuse images and child luring.

The mandate of the NCECC is to reduce the vulnerability of children to internet-facilitated sexual exploitation by identifying victimized children; investigating and assisting in the prosecution of sexual offenders; and, strengthening the capacity of municipal, territorial, provincial, federal, and international police agencies through training and investigative support.

The NCECC mandate was built on the G8 objectives for protecting children from sexual exploitation on the internet and these objectives guide the work of the NCECC:

• Victim Identification
• Suspect Location
• International Cooperation
• Law Enforcement: Tools and Training
• Awareness and Prevention
• Intelligence/Information: Gather, Disseminate, and Share

- Non-Government/Industry Cooperation
- Legislation

The Centre provides a number of services to law enforcement, including the ability to respond immediately to a child at risk, the coordination of investigative files, expertise in victim identification techniques, management of multi-jurisdictional cases, operationally relevant research, and training specific to online child sexual exploitation investigations. The NCECC also manages and provides training for the Child Exploitation Tracking System (CETS), an intelligence tool that enhances information sharing among investigators.

CETS is a software program that assists in managing and linking worldwide child protection cases across jurisdictions, by providing tools for gathering and sharing evidence and information on those who commit crimes against children. The program was developed by Microsoft Corporation at the request of, and in collaboration with, the Toronto Police Service in Canada in 2003. Since its inception, law enforcement agencies in countries around the world have adopted the CETS tool.

A synopsis of the statistics in Table 1 following indicates:

- In 2009 there were over 50,000 cases of children registered as missing with the RCMP Missing Children's Registry in Ottawa.
- In 2009 there were 10,348 children registered missing from British Columbia.
- The greatest number of these children had run away from home—4,757 children in 2009—and most returned within forty-eight hours. There are no words to describe the anguish for the parents of those children who don't.
- Thirty-seven British Columbia children were kidnapped by one of their parents, usually in the heat of a divorce or custody battle.
- In 2009 there were sixteen British Columbia children who went missing as a result of kidnapping or foul play.

All statistics courtesy of the RCMP Missing Children's Registry.

Table 1

Total 2009 Missing Children Reports by Province and Profile

Profile	YT	NT	NU	BC	AB	SK	MB	ON	QC	NB	PE	NS	NL	Totals
Stranger	0	0	0	16	6	1	3	11	7	2	0	1	3	50
Accident	0	0	0	6	1	2	0	11	1	0	0	0	4	25
Wandered	0	0	0	94	64	18	24	209	12	2	0	8	1	432
Parental	0	1	0	37	13	14	16	94	56	2	1	3	1	237
Runaway	3	11	0	4,757	4,456	2,149	3,435	13,634	5,183	618	20	1,336	166	35,768
Unknown	2	5	0	4,759	573	779	730	3,065	1,638	58	5	75	68	11,757
Other	0	3	0	679	59	30	38	835	518	4	1	51	5	2,223
Totals	**5**	**19**	**0**	**10,348**	**5,172**	**2,993**	**4,246**	**17,859**	**7,415**	**686**	**27**	**1,474**	**248**	**50,492**

Canadian Police Center for Missing and Exploited Children National Missing Children Services,
National Police Services, Royal Canadian Mounted Police

Table 2
Canadian Missing Children Reports Summary
CPIC Year-end Transaction Reports for 2008
Frequency by Category and by Year Reported Missing

Profile	Kidnap	PA	Run	Unknown	Acc	Wander	Other	Total
2009	50	237	35,768	11,757	25	432	2,223	50,492
2008	56	300	40,289	12,441	37	560	2,419	56,102
2007	56	285	46,189	11,216	33	576	2,227	60,582
2006	46	326	46,728	10,761	24	567	2,009	60,461
2005	30	349	51,280	12,079	45	704	2,061	66,548
2004	31	332	52,280	11,373	27	671	2,552	67,266
2003	39	358	53,459	10,922	21	805	2,205	67,809
2002	35	429	52,390	10,994	38	594	2,052	66,532
2001	48	387	53,434	10,364	49	742	1,990	66,994
2000	42	416	50,633	10,031	35	597	1,958	63,712
1999	52	358	47,585	9,884	38	496	1,947	60,360
1998	42	426	48,388	10,254	28	623	2,326	62,087
1997	60	426	45,527	9,404	37	506	2,138	58,098
1996	45	409	43,717	9,181	34	822	1,914	56,122
1995	68	354	43,709	9,039	35	720	1,824	55,749

Kidnap= kidnapping/stranger abduction

PA=parental abduction

Run=runaways

Acc= accident

Wander =wandered off (when a child is presumed to have wandered away and not returned when expected)

Other=when a child has not returned to a detention home or institution housing a young offender

Appendix IV

Missing Children's Day in the United States — The Etan Patz Story

In 1983, President Ronald Reagan proclaimed May 25th as National Missing Children's Day after a series of high-profile missing-children cases led to a nationwide awareness of child abduction, and the shocking lack of resources and plans devoted to solving crimes against children. The first of those cases was six-year-old Etan Patz, who disappeared in New York City on May 25, 1979 and has never been found. His disappearance drew national attention to the lack of coordinated procedures to address child abduction, and influenced modern procedures for locating missing children. Etan's was the first photo of a missing child to be printed on the back of milk cartons.

On the morning of his disappearance, Etan, wearing his favourite captain's hat, kissed his mother goodbye on the sidewalk outside their downtown Manhattan apartment and headed towards the bus stop two blocks away to catch the school bus. It was the first time he had been allowed to walk the short distance on his own. It was later discovered that he never made it to the bus stop and was not in school all that day.

When he failed to return home that afternoon, his mother reported him missing and an intense search began, involving neighbours, over one hundred police officers and a team of bloodhounds. The quest to find Etan continued for weeks, with missing-child posters everywhere throughout the city and photos of him projected onto screens in Times Square.

Etan's case brought forth numerous crank calls, a medium that had strange visions, an extortionist, and the ongoing invasion of the Patz family home by the news media and the police. It was all documented in files kept by Etan's father, Stan, and later used in a book written by Lisa Cohen in 2009 entitled, *After Etan: The Missing Child Case that Held America Captive.*

After several years, a convicted pedophile named Jose Antonio Ramos became the prime suspect in the case. It was learned he had been acquainted with a woman who had worked as a babysitter for the Patzes and that in May 1979 he lived in a tenement building on the east side, about a mile from where the Patzes resided. He was implicated in several child abuse cases over the years, but always managed to evade charges, until finally being convicted of child molestation in 1987 for a case against two young boys, and then again for another case in 1990, while still serving the sentence from his earlier conviction.

Stuart GraBois, a federal prosecutor who dedicated his life to solving the Patz case, attempted by every means possible to get Ramos to confess to abducting Etan; but although Ramos admitted to bringing a boy who looked like Etan to his apartment on that day, he insisted he had let him go. Two different informers were even planted in Ramos' cell in prison, and each later told investigators similar stories: that Ramos had boasted about his exploits with young boys and had even given details of his abuse of Etan Patz. But when confronted with his "admissions" he denied everything.

Investigators maintained that although Ramos had on occasion come close to incriminating himself in the Patz case, they never had enough evidence to charge him with a crime.

Meanwhile, Ramos also set up his own web page while in prison on which he offered insight into the missing boy's fate. "As to what actually happened to Etan Patz," wrote Ramos, "if any freedom-loving American wants the true story, I kindly ask that you send $2 to my snail-mail address."

In 1999, in a special feature on missing children that appeared in the *New York Post*, Ramos was publicly declared the prime suspect in Etan's disappearance. Without sufficient evidence, however, the authorities were still unable to prosecute him.

In 2001, Etan was declared legally dead, and Etan's parents pursued a civil case against Ramos. In 2004, Justice Barbara R. Kapnick pronounced that Jose A. Ramos was responsible for the death of Etan Patz and granted a judgement in the wrongful death lawsuit by the Patz family against Ramos. Etan's parents were awarded a "symbolic" sum of $2 million, none of which they have ever collected.

Every year on both the anniversaries of Etan's birthday and his disappearance, Stan Patz sends Ramos a copy of his son's missing poster, on the back of which he always types the same message: "What did you do to my little boy?"

Ramos is currently serving a twenty-year prison term for child molestation in the State Correctional Institute in Dallas, Pennsylvania; his scheduled release date is November 7, 2012.

On May 25, 2010, Manhattan District Attorney Cyrus Vance Jr. officially re-opened the Etan Patz case. In April 2012, the FBI and the NYPD excavated a basement property near the Patz' home in the Soho district, which had been the workshop and storage space of a carpenter who had lived in the neighborhourhood at one time, and apparently had been newly refurbished soon after Etan's disappearance. After a four-day search, investigators announced that they had found "nothing conclusive, including no skeletal or human remains."

Then, on May 24, 2012, the New York Police Commissioner announced that Pedro Hernandez of Maple Shade, New Jersey had confessed to strangling Etan, and he was charged with second-degree murder. However, his lawyer has stated that Hernandez has a history of mental illness including hallucinations. Despite previous confessions to family and church members that he had killed a young boy and put the body in the trash, FBI officials and the police were still doubtful about Hernandez' confession because of its many inconsistencies. There was also no physical evidence linking Hernandez to the crime.

The disappearance and possible murder of Etan Patz remains a mystery.

Appendix V
Children's Bill of Rights as Developed by Child Find

You have the right to:

Learn and ask questions

•

Seek help

•

Laugh and be happy

•

Express your feelings

•

Take care of yourself

•

Follow your dreams

•

Do things for yourself

•

Protect your mind and body

•

Receive and give affection

•

Be proud of your work

•

Be the best you can be

•

Love yourself, love others and be loved

Appendix VI
Child Find Offices Across Canada

Child Find BC
Tel: (250) 382-7311
Fax: (250) 382-0227
Email: childvicbc@shaw.ca

Child Find Alberta
Tel: (403) 270-3463
Fax: (403) 270-8355
Provincial Toll Free: 1-800-561-1733
Email: childfindalberta@storehouse39.ca

Child Find Saskatchewan
Tel: (306) 955-0070
Fax: (306) 373-1311
Email: childsask@aol.com

Child Find Manitoba
Tel: (204) 945-5735
Fax:(204) 948-2461
Email: childmb@aol.com

Child Find Ontario
Tel: (905) 712-3463
Fax: (905) 712-3462
Toll Free: 1-866-543-8477
Email: mail@childfindontario.ca

Child Find Nova Scotia
Tel: (902) 454-2030
Fax: (902) 429-6749
Toll Free: 1-800-682-9006
Email: childfindns@aol.com

Child Find PEI
Tel: (902) 368-1678
Fax: (902) 368-1389
Email: childfind@pei.aibn.com

Child Find Newfoundland and Labrador
Tel: (709) 738-4400
Fax: (709) 738-0550
Email: childfindnfld@aol.com

Child Find Canada
Tel: (204) 339-5584
Fax: (204) 339-5587
Email: childcan@aol.com

For Quebec, Yukon, Nunavut and the North West Territories,
Contact Child Find Canada above.

Bibliography

Black, Bonnie. 1981. *Somewhere Child.* Viking Press, New York.

Cohen, Lisa R. 2009. *After Etan: The Missing Child Case that Held America Captive.* Grand Central Publishing, New York.

Dugard, Jaycee Lee. 2011. *A Stolen Life.* Simon & Schuster, New York, NY.

Fass, Paula S. 2006. *Kidnapped: Child Abduction in America.* Oxford University Press, New York, NY.

Gill, John E. 1982. *Stolen Children.* Penguin Press, New York.

Green, Valerie. 2011. *Mysterious British Columbia: Myths, Murders, Mysteries and Legends.* Quagmire Press Ltd. Edmonton, Alberta.

Greene, Marilyn. 1990. *Finder: The True Story of a Private Investigator.* Simon & Shuster, New York.

Virk, Manjit. 2009 *Rena: A Father's Story.* Heritage House Publishing, Victoria, BC.

Wojna, Lisa. 2007. *Missing: The Disappeared, Lost or Abducted in Canada.* Quagmire Press Ltd., Edmonton, Alberta.

Websites

www.missingkids.ca

www.michaeldunahee.ca

www.lindseyslaw.ca

Sources

Chapter One
- Victoria City Police: interview with detectives
- Victoria City Police website: www.vicpd.ca
- Crystal and Bruce Dunahee: interviews, July to December 2011

Chapter Two
- Child Find BC website: www.childfindbc.com
- Victoria Police Department: interviews
- Federal Bureau of Investigation website: www.fbi.gov

Chapter Three
- Victoria Police Department: interviews
- RCMP website: www.rcmp-grc.ca

Chapter Four
- Scott Johnson: interviews and emails Oct/Nov/Dec 2011
- Crystal Dunahee: interview September 2011
- *Victoria Times Colonist:* articles, March 1992
- *Esquimalt News:* "Pleasants' Pen" March 25, 1992
- *Esquimalt News:* "Letters to the Editor" March 1992

Chapter Five
- Steve Orcherton, Director of Child Find BC: interview, August 2011 and subsequent correspondence

Chapter Six
- John Carlow: email correspondence, August to November 2011
- Missing Childrens' Society website: www.childsearch.org

Chapter Seven
- Victoria Police Department: interview
- Crystal Dunahee: interviews
- National Centre for Missing & Exploited Children: correspondence
- Age-Enhancing Artists Information through correspondence. (NCMEC)

Chapter Eight
- *Globe & Mail:* article by Tom Hawthorne, March 2011
- www.michaeldunahee.ca
- www.missingchildren.ca

Chapter Nine
- Caitlin Dunahee: interview, September 24, 2011 and subsequent correspondence
- Facebook page: *We Will never Forget Michael Dunahee*

Chapter Ten
- Karen Dunahee: interview, October 15, 2011
- Dorothy Arsenault: correspondence, November/December 2011

Chapter Eleven
- Websites: Elizabeth Smart, Jaycee Dugard, Kienan Heibert
- *Victoria Times Colonist:* "Kidnapped boy returned after two years." Dec.18, 1993
- *Victoria Times Colonist:* December 2011
- Missing Children's Society website: www.childsearch.org

Conclusion
- Victoria Police Department

Index

age-enhanced photo development, 84–86
Alexa, Ben, 16
AMBER Alert, 103, 109, 131–3
America's Most Wanted, 25–27, 34–36, 45, 55, 59, 61
Archie Browning Centre, 89
Arsenault,
  Chris, 23
  Cody, 105
  Dorothy, 23, 80, 105–107, 156
  Jordan, 105

Baswick, Daryl (detective), 158
BCTV (now Global), 41
Behavioral Sciences Unit (BSU), 24–25
Bennett, David, 42
Bland, Don (detective), 36, 90, 158
Boland, Diana, 92
Brown, Sylvia, 59–60
Brooks, Garth, 104

Camosun College, 21
Canadian Centre for Child Protection, 92, 109, 111, 118
Canon Cameras, 54, 156
Carlow, John, 55–58, 61–62, 64, 154, 159
Cedar Hill Recreation Centre, 40, 72
CFAX Radio, 40
Chase, BC, 91–92
Chase, Bonnie, 89
CHEK TV, 18, 40, 59
Child Exploitation Tracking System (CETS), 144
Chisholm,
  Joe, 116, 119
  Stephanie (pseudonym), 116–120
Christensen, Wendy, 119
CJVI Radio (now JACK FM), 40
CKDA Radio (defunct), 40
Cochrane, Al (detective), 86, 158
Cooper, Denise Etchart, 44

Davis, Richard Allen, 61–62

Dini Petty Show, 58
DNA, 109–111, 135
Donair Shop, 89, 102
Ducker, John (deputy chief), 120, 158
Dunahee,
  Barbara, 18, 21, 52, 105
  Bruce, 15, 21, 25, 38, 79–80, 101, 154
  Caitlin, 49, 78, 95, 99, 155
  Crystal, 15, 30, 42, 52, 54, 81, 89, 94, 101, 112, 121, 130, 154–155
  Harvey, 38, 104
  Karen, 103, 155
  Keith, 21–22
Dugard, Jaycee, 113, 155

Easter, Wayne, Solicitor General, 101
Esquimalt News, The, 43
Esquimalt Recreation Centre, 46–47, 93, 99

Federal Bureau of Investigation (FBI), 23
Fleming, Rob, 108
Focus on Women, 60
Fort Francis, Ontario, 21
Fouracres, Laurie, 89
Fox,
  Betty, 124
  Terry, 124

Gabereau, Vicki, 64
Gehl, Bob (inspector), 91, 158
Geraldo, 59–60
GPS, 133–134
Greene, Marilyn, 56
Grusser, Wilbert, 115–116

Hawthorne, Tom, 90, 155
Harper, Stephen, Prime Minister, 77, 92
Hebert, Kienan, 113–114
Hellcats, 15, 38, 46, 102
Homemakers (magazine), 60
Hopley, Randall, 113–114

Jeffries,
  Crystal, 21
  Family, 83
Jenks, Mavis, 73, 83
Johnson, Scott, 39, 46, 49, 72, 154, 159

Kevin Collins Foundation, 44, 61
KlaasKids Foundation, 63
Klaas,
  Marc, 62
  Polly, 61–63
Kwantlen Polytechnic University, 99

Larry King Live, 63
Lindner, Keith (inspector), 158
Lindsey's Law, 110
Lunn, Gary, 110

Maclean's Magazine, 60
Michelle Remembers, 26–27
Missing Children's Day, 54, 92, 109, 147
Missing Children's Society of Canada (MCSC), 56, 117
Monk Office Supply, 41
Monue, Harry, 59
Morgan, Rhonda, 56

Nancy Grace Show, 63
National Child Exploitation Co-ordination Centre, 143–144
National Center for Missing and Exploited Children (NCMEC), 53, 57, 85, 114
Nicholson, Rob, 92
Nicholls, Lindsey, 110
NorthWest Afternoon, 59
North Island College, 103

O'Bryne, Patricia, 117, 119–120
Oliphant, Gordon, 42
Oprah, 59, 60
Orcherton,
  Peg, 108
  Steve, 8, 28, 49, 51, 52, 54, 77–79, 108, 154, 158
Orr, Sheila, 108
Our Lady Queen of Peace Church, 15, 38

Patz,
  Etan, 147–149
  Stan, 149
People, 60
Peterson, Judy, 109–110
Pezim, Murray, 28
Pioneer Co-Operative Housing Complex, 15
Point, Steven, Lt. Governor, 94
Port McNeil, 92

Ramos, Jose A., 149
Ravensdale, Henry, 42
RCMP Missing Children's Registry, 57, 144
Reagan, Ronald, President, 147
Rice, Ray (mayor), 49
Rinaldo, Sandie, 58
Ryder, Winona, 61–63

Satory, Arped, 42
Schools
  Blanshard Elementary, 16, 25, 42, 70, 101, 103
  Brentwood Bay Elementary, 48
  Esquimalt High, 21, 22, 39
  Lake Hill Elementary, 48
  Lampson Elementary, 21
  Macaulay Elementary, 48
  Rock Hill Elementary, 21
Seitz, Vernon, 87
Shoppers Drug Mart, 41
Smart, Elizabeth, 112, 155
Smith, John (detective), 28, 158
Soles, Linden, 41–42, 72

Tournament of Hope, 53, 78, 81
Tree of Hope, 42, 74, 101

Victoria General Hospital, 83
Victoria Times-Colonist, 23

Walsh,
  Adam, 25
  John, 25, 45, 59
Waxman, Al, 58
Wood, Anthony, 92

Acknowledgements

Without the complete co-operation of, and assistance from, the Dunahee family, this book would not have been possible. First and foremost, I therefore wish to sincerely thank Crystal, Bruce and Caitlin, and their extended family, for answering numerous questions and offering me the help I needed. I especially appreciate the fact that they were willing to open up their hearts and share their tragic story with me. After over two decades of being exposed to endless media attention, this re-hashing of the story yet again must not have been easy for them.

My thanks and admiration also goes to the officers of the Victoria Police Department for their ongoing determination to solve a case that has seemed unsolvable. The following are just a few of the many officers involved in Michael's case through the years:

Detective John Smith, Detective Al Cochrane, Detective Don Bland, Detective Daryl Baswick, Inspector Keith Lindner, Inspector Bob Gehl and Deputy Chief John Ducker. There were also many other dedicated officers, too numerous to individually mention by name, but who all worked around the clock on Michael's case. If all their names were to be included in these acknowledgements, it would fill the entire book. Michael's disappearance is still an active, open case, and will remain so until the determined officers who are still working the case find answers. My thanks also go to the Victoria Police Department's research and identity departments.

In addition, I wish to acknowledge the help of Steve Orcherton of Child Find BC. Thanks also to the National Center for Missing and Exploited Children for the age-enhanced photographs of Michael. Special thanks to retired Chief Superintendent Kate Lines of the Ontario Police Dept. (OPD) for her interest, insight and support; and special appreciation to John Carlow and to the Missing Children's Society. I also wish to acknowledge the countless volunteers who have helped in the search for Michael through the years. Their dedication is commendable.

And a big debt of gratitude to Scott Johnson for his input and photographic material. To my friend Joan Neudecker, I offer my thanks for sharing many old newspaper clippings with me. And thank you, Terry, for the initial connection to start this incredible ball rolling.

Thanks also to Hancock House Publishers for understanding the importance of this story and especially to editor Theresa Laviolette who was a pleasure to work with.

And finally, as always, I thank my husband David for allowing me the time, space and his never-ending support to enable me to write this very special story which has been close to my heart for so many years.

About the Author

Valerie Green was born in England and studied journalism, English literature and history at the Regent Institute of Journalism in London. Before immigrating to Canada in 1968, Valerie's employment included a stint at the War Office for MI5, as well as legal secretarial work and freelance writing. Her writing career is extensive and includes writing a weekly history column for the *Saanich News* for nineteen years, numerous articles for the *Victoria Times Colonist,* as well as authoring sixteen books on local and regional history, mysteries and social issues.

Now semi-retired, Valerie continues to write a monthly column for the *Seaside Times* in Sidney, and to freelance for a number of newspapers and magazines. In addition, she serves on the board of the Saanich Arts, Culture & Heritage Committee and volunteers with the Luther Court Society. She is a member of the Professional Writers of Canada (PWAC), the Federation of BC Writers, the Writers' Union of Canada, and the Hallmark Society of Victoria.

She lives with her husband and their dog, Rupert, in Saanich. Visit her website at www.valeriegreen.ca/